Capturing
MEMORIES

The Art of Reminiscing

Capturing MEMORIES

The Art of Reminiscing

VIVIENNE WOOLF **JEANIE ROSEFIELD**
PAT STANTON **SUE GORDON**

Foreword
MAUREEN LIPMAN

VALLENTINE MITCHELL
LONDON • PORTLAND, OR

First published in 2002 in Great Britain by
VALLENTINE MITCHELL
Crown House, 47 Chase Side, Southgate
London N14 5BP

and in the United States of America by
VALLENTINE MITCHELL
c/o ISBS, 5824 N.E. Hassalo Street
Portland, Oregon, 97213-3644

Website: www.vmbooks.com

British Library Cataloguing in Publication Data

ISBN 0-85303-440-0 (paper)

Library of Congress Cataloging-in-Publication Data

A catalog record for this book is available
from the Library of Congress

Typeset in Garamond Bold 11/14pt by Cambridge Photosetting Services,
Cambridge
Printed in Great Britain by MPG Books Ltd, Bodmin, Cornwall

Contents

To our children: Vivienne's James and John; Jeanie's Laura, Jayne and Gemma; Pat's Lara, David, Ilana and Sarah; Sue's Sarah and Jane; and to all young people who will one day have memories of their own to share.

List of Illustrations

14. There were always ways of getting around rationing. *Hackney Gazette*, 16 December 1946.
15. Whom did Anne phone? Her mother, of course.
16. Schevzik's in Brick Lane were Russian Vapour Baths where men went to *schwitz* (sweat). Tuesday was ladies' day.
17. Two young boys shaved clean to the scalp either to cure or prevent nits.
18. Patent medicines were popular for many ailments; and the fad for 'slimming' pills has a long history.
19. A visit to a real dentist was a 'luxury' that few East Enders could afford. *Hackney Official Guide*, c. 1915.
20. For those whose rooms and beds were *lunzen mit vanzen* Keatings Powder provided one – temporary! – solution. 1939.
21. From the British Home and Colonial Furniture Stores catalogue, showing the wardrobes, dressing tables and chests that were in style during the 1930s.
22. Proper pyjamas and nightdresses were only affordable by the better off. These pure silk pyjamas would have been an unheard-of luxury for most people. *The Queen*, 5 May 1943.
23. Gambling posed a real problem for families who were already struggling to exist on meagre incomes. 1936.
24. Efforts at maintaining a 'public face' were not always successful. *Hackney Gazette*, 1938.
25. The soup kitchen for the Jewish poor in Brune Street – now a luxury block of flats.
26. *Hackney Gazette*, March 1922.
27. The 'Monkey Parade' aroused much moral concern among the more traditional members of the Jewish community. *The Jewish Chronicle*, 15 March 1929.
28. Joe Coral worked his way up from runner for illegal bookies to owner of the largest chain of betting shops in the UK.
29. Derby Day, 1936. Gypsies, tipsters (including Prince Monolulu, to the left), hawkers and entertainers at Epsom for the famous race.
30. Second-hand clothes could be bought at Cheepen, 32 Bath Street, Clerkenwell, EC1.
31. The 'Black Market' flourished during the War. *Hackney Gazette*, 16 January 1948.

32. Abraham Smith's butcher shop, 68 Brushfield Street. (His previous premises in Princes Street, Spitalfields, had burnt down.)
33. D. Ackerman & Sons jewellery shop, 11 Greenfield Street.
34. M. Boxer Wholesale Provision Merchant.
35. Joe Loss was one of the most popular band leaders of the 1940s.
36. An advertisement for the Holborn Empire, The Regent at Stamford Hill, and the Hackney Empire Theatre, shows the wide range of entertainment available in the late 1920s. *North London Recorder*, 31 May 1929.
37. Harry Finn in the Norwood JLB band, 1926.
38. The Oxford and St George's Club in Berner Street, E1, was one of the many youth clubs set up with the intent of keeping young boys off the streets. This is a postcard addressed to Mrs Phillips in Orchid Road, N14, showing (back row) Jack R., Ben A., Jack G., R.W., and Scholy; (front row) Willie S., Ike G., M.O.S., Alf G., and Ben D.
39. The strong moral and religious purposes behind youth clubs is made clear in this letter from Lily Montagu (d. 22 January 1963). This letter was found after her death and was addressed to her club members.
40. A 'charabanc' outing to Westcliffe. Everyone sat in the square overlooking the sea by the toilets opposite the tea stall, *not* on the beach.
41. An advertisement from the 1930s for the 'most luxuriously furnished Jewish Hotel in the United Kingdom'.
42. Ann and Sam Boxer enjoy a day at the seaside. Note the attire!
43. Although shops were frequently close to home many, such as S. Waterman & Sons, would deliver orders to your door.
44. Lyons were the most famous tea houses in London.
45. Kosher restaurants could be hired out for weddings.
46. Reminiscence groups provide a valuable opportunity for the old and young to share their experiences.
47. Members of the North East London Day Centre Stamford Hill in the Reminiscence Room.
48. Reminiscence groups can be an important source of information for the young on their community's cultural heritage.
49. A Reminiscence Room can contain a wide range of familiar items, including wedding dresses, menorahs, and a *genzunder*.

Acknowledgements

A list of people in the groups at the Michael Sobell Community Centre, the Stamford Hill Community Centre and the Sinclair House Day Centre who so generously gave their stories:

Stamford Hill Community Centre and the Sinclair House Day Centre

Harry Abrahams
Leila Abrahams
Hilda Allen
Jean Allen
Sam Altman
Lionel Brodie
Philippa Broer
John Burdess
Gerald Cohen
Fay Conway
Rose Crown
Lilly de Bruin
Ben Ellerman

Debbie Faith
Harry Finn
Anita Frankley
Colin Freeman
Ray Goldstein
Rita Gordon
Peter Haagman
Ray Jelen
Lilly Jesner
Beattie Judah
Wally Kalb
Rose Lee
Louis Levene

Hetty Mason
Bertha Moss
Issie Neville
Tilly Neville
Terry Pearlman
Lilly Philips
Maurice Pordes
Louis Rolnick
Alfred Simpkin
Ezekial Sion
Eve Summers
Millie Tucker

The Michael Sobell Community Centre:

Millie Bojm
Sadie Berkowitz
Fay Clarke
Barbara Cohen

Mary Conway
Barney Donner
Louis Feldman
Tilly Fentom

Pearl Forman
Vera Foster
Marie Gelblem
Anne Gerson

S. Gibesh

Betty Green

Morris Green

Jack Greene

Marlene Hadjizade

Gloria Harris

Rose Hecht

David Hoffman

Blanche Hyams

June Jocum

Rosina Kaye

Lizzie Lebby

Nat Lee

Sara Lee

Dora Leigh

Lila Leigh

Julie Levy

Rachel Levy

Pearl Marks

Elsie Peltz

Maurice Peltz

Elie Reitman

Lily Rivers

Nora Robart

Miriam Saberski

Annette Saville

Bernard Sefton

Doris Sewell

Maurice Simons

Lily Silver

Pearl Slater

Godfrey Solomons

Rene Solomons

Abie Steinberg

We are also grateful to Anne Futter for the time and effort she put into preparing the topic boxes, to John Rosefield for taking the marvellous photograph for the front cover and the photographs of some of the group members in the reminiscence rooms, and to Clare Hawtin for her invaluable practical help in assembling the manuscript.

Preface

This is not a history book.

Recalling a special memory from the past is a creative process and not necessarily an accurate one. The memory is recreated each time it is told by the person who holds it, yet can be slightly different with each telling. The images or events seem to be like little piles of autumn leaves beneath a tree. The mind is that tree and each leaf is the memory of the event that is saved from destruction by the relating of the memory to other people. Each leaf from the pile brings a very different memory to life.

A lingering gaze at the photograph of your grandfather may be a reminder of the way his beard tickled as he kissed you, the way he swayed when he prayed, or even the trips to the cinema and the monkey nuts that he shared with you. Others in the family may have a different memory of his face, character and life. Reminiscing with others and sharing their differing piles of leaves – or thoughts – revives and recaptures memories that were long since forgotten.

Foreword

This book brought many childhood memories alive for me. I remember, for example, the women of my childhood – the indomitable, varied, never-changing and constant women – the Fredas, the Noras, the Lillys, the Minnies – women who were as smart as paint. These women were happy comparing their kids and watching their husbands make a living and shopping daily on what he gave them weekly and socialising with each other at synagogue functions and barmitzvahs and silver weddings. They married in utility suits and borrowed hats and the men they married donned uniforms and left within weeks or months of their ration-book weddings. In their quiet moments all of them feared that the uniformed strangers who might return would do so with new manners and new mores to which they may not know how to rise. I remember the companionable vivacity, the shared jokes and the pooled fears. I remember the pride that only a wage-packet with your name on it could bring. Our mothers knew that their place was in the home so when we came home from school clutching our 'could do better if she stopped trying to entertain the class' report, they gave us beans on toast and a homemade macaroon. Nowadays, when asked the question 'What in your roles has inspired you?' I see etched on my retina these women who would never achieve what we today could achieve, but by hell were going to make sure that their Maureens and Susans and Charles did.

I wish more people had the same opportunities as those who gave their stories for this book. Their memories enrich our lives and our Jewish heritage and their encouragement and love inspired their families to succeed. We value their contribution.

Maureen Lipman
London
2001

Introduction

A group was talking together about the East End markets. A lady said, 'Let me tell you a thing or two about the rogues in the markets. You had to be very careful not to be cheated. Buying shoes without laces or pairs of seamed stockings where only one stocking was seamed was not unusual in those days.' An elderly man sheepishly admitted that he was once a market trader and often sold mismatched pairs of stockings to unsuspecting customers. The room filled with raucous laughter, wagging fingers and cries of 'Lobus, you old rascal!' The one-time trader beamed with delight at the reaction to his confession and reminiscence was on its way!

1. Surprises bring laughter to a group.

1

Reminiscence is more than a friendly chat. Special skills are needed to draw people out, to enable them to focus on a topic in depth and reap the benefits of being part of a group. The lifeline of shared heritage binds people together within and beyond the group. People develop insights into each other's personalities and interests; they have fun, laughter and tears, emerging with a greater sense of self-worth.

Reminiscence is a two-way process between young and old. The young benefit from the wisdom learned of experience. Older people are encouraged by enthusiasm and stimulated by discussion to give and to feel validated.

In the following chapters we share with you insights from the lives of Jewish people in London between the Wars based purely on memories revealed through reminiscence. These group memories bring a special perspective and a unique contribution to our knowledge of social history, and of our Jewish heritage. These are the memories of the historians of yesteryear.

The Good Old Days

Dear Brother or Sister, whilst seeking the truth
Of years that have gone with its valiant youth,
Let's tell of a story of pleasures long past,
And the glory of living and love that can last

Much love for our parents, each neighbour a guest,
All serving one purpose and that was the best.
We rarely had plenty, the going was rough,
We lived through an age when enough was enough.

As parents deciding the right way to live
We took all life offered, all life had to give.
And as age followed age we all had to learn
Of the life yet to come but would never return.

Whatever life offered we took with a smile,
We struggled together for mile after mile,
But as age follows youth in its cumbersome way
Thank God we're all happy to be here today.

Nat Lee

On Being Jewish

An awareness of 'how Jewish you felt' came in different ways. Some of the people we spoke to said that their sense of Jewish identity depended simply upon the community or street in which they lived. Other people 'felt Jewish' because their grandmothers told them they were so; because their grandfathers had big white beards; because their mothers used 'white cloths on Friday nights'; because they had *mezzuzot* (scrolls containing a handwritten prayer) fixed to their doorposts; because they were forbidden to eat jellied eels or because their parents spoke 'broken English fluently'. One man knew he must be Jewish because his Jewish relatives and friends pinched his cheeks and called him *bubbele* ('sweetie') and another knew of his Jewish identity because his family ate only chickens that were 'killed in a certain way' in the markets. A lady knew she was different because her father, the proud, bearded *chazan* in their largely non-Jewish community had to walk to synagogue flanked by two good friends from the Salvation Army, there to protect him from taunts and ' flying tomatoes.'

In the East End of London, most of your neighbours were likely to be Jewish and Yiddish was the language most frequently heard. Mothers would call out in Yiddish for their children to come in off the streets for their supper. The children who were often acutely embarrassed answered back: '*Mama, redden nicht Yiddish mit mir*'; which means 'Mother, don't speak Yiddish with me.' Notwithstanding this, the Jewish mother – the 'Yiddishe Mama' as the Sophie Tucker song went – left an imprint which forever

5

shaped her children's lives: 'I don't remember my mama as ever being young. She was always tired and working;' 'No exertion was too much for her. She regarded her children as her jewels and better than money;' 'This *'heimische* Frau' brought foreign ways to London life;' 'She did not often show emotion or affection by cuddling but she showed her love in the way she worked ceaselessly to care for us;' 'She treated us as if we were kings and queens;' 'She suffered in silence – however difficult father could be;' 'A chip off the old block;' 'A goddess.' When times were hard, she wisely counselled, 'This too, shall pass' and although she sometimes told her children to 'forget religion – just be good,' she ensured that all her children, the boys particularly, were educated in Hebrew and in English so that they could both perpetuate their religious traditions and be integrated into the world at large.

Of course, Hebrew learning was just a part of being Jewish. There was *Shabbat* (the Sabbath) when 'for some strange reason, living was different;' there were the festivals that seemed to follow on so closely one from another that 'you could not get away from them;' and the indefinable something called 'heritage' or 'tradition' that was in your blood.

As far as Jewish education was concerned, children either attended Jewish schools or received their Jewish education in the *cheder* classes that formed a focus in their neighbourhoods. In some areas, there were as many as two or three of these so-called *chedorim* on each street and they varied considerably in quality. Some were regarded as seedy places and some, such as the one on Shacklewell Lane, were remembered with affection. A one-time pupil described his education at Shacklewell Lane in Dalston as 'stunning.' The more observant members of the community might send their children to Talmud Torahs to receive a Jewish education. These Talmud Torahs were regarded, on the whole, as the best possible path to religious education and two of the most popular were situated on Redmond Road and Christian Street. Talmud Torahs were known to perform acts of charity towards the poor in the community such as distributing *matzos* (unleavened bread) during the festival of Passover. Some parents sent their children to study privately with a *melamed* (a man 'of learning'), rather than have

Redmans Road Talmud Torah.

LADIES' SOCIETY'S SEMI-JUBILEE.

A dinner in celebration of the twenty-fifth anniversary of the Redmans Road Talmud Torah Ladies' Society was held, last Saturday evening, at the La Bohème Ballrooms, Mile End Road. Mrs. J. H. HERTZ presided, in the absence of Mrs. I. M. Sieff, and in proposing the toast of the Ladies' Society, said that the Society provided food and clothing for the needy children. and marked the Jewish Festivals by giving the children little treats and extras. For the last three years the Three C's (Combined Charities Committee) had given that Talmud Torah the proceeds of some of its functions and had enabled the Ladies' Society to pay for the text-books used in the classes. The use of text books with large clear type, would earn the gratitude of the Jewish Health Organisation, which made the eyesight of Jewish children its special care. It was only right that on that evening they should recall the names of those women, some of whom were no longer with them, who helped to organise and steer that Society during the early days of its existence. Mrs. H. Chissick was the first President of the Society. Mrs. Milgrom was a Vice-President whose main work was that of investigating the cases of needy children. Mrs. Rabbinovitch also a Vice-President, distinguished herself at a time of food shortage by collecting the necessary food for the children's meals. In conclusion Mrs. Hertz paid a tribute to the work of Mesdames Hyams, President, Portugal and Newfield, Vice-Presidents, Steinberg and Cissie Hyams.

Rabbi M. RABBINOWITZ responded to the toast of the Ladies' Society.

The Rev. J. K. GOLDBLOOM, Principal of the Talmud Torah, presented an illuminated address, on behalf of the Honorary Officers of the Talmud Torah, to the Honorary Officers of the Ladies' Society. The address will be hung in the Board Room of the Talmud Torah and copies will be presented to each Honorary Officer of the Ladies' Society. Mr. Goldbloom said that there were 550 children attending the Talmud Torah, and referred to the precarious financial position of the London Talmud Torahs and *Yeshibot*. He appealed for support of the Redmans Road Talmud Torah which was in debt for several hundred pounds. Mr. Goldbloom paid a tribute to the work of the Ladies' Society, and said that much valuable assistance had been rendered to the Institution by Mrs. A. Levin (the wife of a Vice-President of the Talmud Torah) assisted by Mr. Myer Loshack, who organised a function, as a result of which £250 was handed over to the Talmud Torah.

Mr. S. TEFF, B.A., said that he hoped that every guest present would become a subscriber to the Institution.

Councillor M. H. DAVIS, L.C.C., proposed the toast of the Chairman, and referred to Mrs. Hertz's good work for the community. He would like to inform Mr. Goldbloom that over two years ago the Federation of Synagogues voted £50 to the Yeshiba Etz Chaim for scholarships for two *Talmidim*. He had written and had spoken to prominent officials of the *Yeshiba*, informing them of the decision of the Federation, but they had not yet claimed the money. The offer was still open to them.

Other speakers were Mesdames Portugal, J. Hyams, Cissie Hyams, Messrs. J. Bowman, P. Hyams and Simons. Tributes were paid to the work of the Three C's for their valuable assistance to the Ladies' Society. Messages were read from the Chief Rabbi of the British Empire, Dayan Dr. Feldman, and Mr. A. Mundy.

---

2. Talmud Torahs were an important source of education for the children of the more observant members of the community. *The Jewish Chronicle*, 15 March 1929. [Courtesy of *The Jewish Chronicle*.]

them attend the *chedorim*. These parents preferred to have their children taught by a Yiddish speaker and were prepared to pay for the privilege. Pupils usually sat round the *melamed*'s kitchen table and some complained that their clothes often reeked of the food his wife was cooking! One *melamed* made shoe polish, which he stored in tins in a shed, to supplement his income. The unfortunate man's hands were discoloured and his home smelled. Wherever they were taught, most children learned to read Hebrew and about the festivals, and some studied bible stories and ancient Jewish history. A minority were taught modern Jewish history, but only the dedicated went on to study the Talmud. During the War, children often received religious education by correspondence or, sometimes, were not taught at all.

As far as Jewish education in the wider context was concerned, a lady said that she did not realise she was Jewish until she was sent – at the age of 8 – to Minerva in Leicester, one of the few Jewish boarding schools in England; and another remembered being one of the five Jewish pupils in her school who were ushered into the school hall each day when 'Christian prayers' were over. A man said he 'knew he was Jewish' because he was exempt from writing in classes held during his compulsory Saturday morning school.

The bar mitzvah took place at the age of 13 and was a rite of passage into manhood and religious commitment. This ritual signified the end of Jewish learning for some, the beginning for others, and released most from having to wear short trousers. The more well-to-do parents in the community usually marked this occasion by hosting a small family party at home. Unfortunately, some boys were just too poor to have a bar mitzvah, although most boys in the Norwood home were accorded this privilege. If they were very lucky, boys might receive gifts like Waterman or Platignum fountain pens, watches and Brownie Box cameras. Guests in the synagogue often threw *rozinkes und mandelen* (almonds and raisins) at bar mitzvah boys when they had finished reading their portion of the Torah to encourage them in further study and no harm seemed to come to those who ate these delicacies off the floor. Notwithstanding this, almost every child left Hebrew classes after the bar mitzvah – mostly because they

then entered the work force – and some ceased to attend synagogue regularly except, perhaps, two or three times a year. Some
youngsters were happy to have broken away from the narrow
confines of their communities and some had been turned off
Jewish studies for life by teachers, who sometimes used corporal
punishment and were not happy to be teaching – a fact which they
imprinted on their pupils.

Whatever the extent of their Jewish learning, most community
members' lives were bound by ritual and families usually gathered
together in prayer or social activity on *Shabbat*. Mother cleaned
her home, whitened her doorstep, polished her range with Zebo
black lead polish and began preparing her food on the Thursday
night preceding this holy day. She made her *lockshen* (noodles)
'which she left over chairs to stretch and dry, then chopped up
very quickly into tiny pieces' and her chicken soup. The fowl was
removed from the liquid, roasted and stuffed with chicken fat and
the giblets, and served as a main course on the Friday. In the winter, the dedicated housewives prepared *cholent* (a type of stew
made of meat, potatoes and beans), put it in a pot, covered it with
brown paper and took it to the baker's shop to bake slowly in his
large oven over night. Children were often sent with a ticket to
collect the family *cholent* in time for *Shabbat* lunch. The rabbi's
wife in Booth Street Synagogue made a big *cholent* every week
from which she fed the community's poor. The compassionate
woman turned a blind eye to the non-Jewish tramps who lined
up for some of her food. A lady confessed that when she lived
over a baker's shop, she would creep downstairs on Friday nights
to take a little *cholent* from each of the pots. No one seemed to
notice.

The Yiddishe Mama's main skill lay in making good food 'from
nothing' and she usually cooked and baked with dedication to feed
her family. Some Orthodox homes employed the services of non-
Jewish neighbours on *Shabbat* to perform small chores round the
house and light their fires as they were unable to do so themselves. The less observant in the community often went out to the
cinema, West End, football matches or music halls, where talent
competitions were sometimes held on Friday nights.

9

3. A very rare photograph taken inside Philpott Street Synagogue in the 1920s during the festival of Yom Kippur. Cameras were not usually permitted within a synagogue during services. [Courtesy of Tower Hamlets Archive, Bancroft Road Library.]

Jewish festivals shaped the pattern of communal life and both cooking and food, which was seasonal, were essential to the celebrations. People marked *Rosh Hashanah* (the Jewish New Year) by eating apple, honey, and honey cake for sweetness in the year to come. Some lucky people were able to buy their children new winter clothing, shoes or boots to mark the occasion and most people went to synagogue for at least part of the service. If they did not belong to a synagogue or could not afford to pay membership fees, people could go for no charge to one of the venues, such as cinemas, hired specially for the occasion. On *Yom Kippur* (the Day of Atonement), when people fasted to make reparation for their sins, congregants sometimes passed out in synagogue from exhaustion or hunger and had to be revived by smelling salts. The ladies' gallery often smelled of these salts together with the odour of the mothballs that had protected fur coats worn by the wealthier in the community to mark the day's significance. During the 1930s youngsters sometimes arranged dances to celebrate the end of the fast, but this frivolity often met with rabbis' disapproval.

On *Succot* people ate stuffed vegetables – usually cabbage leaves – and apple strudel; *Shavuot* was the time to bake cheesecake and cheese blintzes; and *Chanukah*, *latkes* (potato pancakes) and doughnuts. Children usually received *Chanukah gelt* (money) a threepenny bit, perhaps, or a sixpence. People sometimes made their own *menorahs* (festive candleholders) for *Chanukah* out of blocks of wood and they lit their candles each night for eight nights as tradition required. On *Purim* some members of the community dressed up in fancy dress, went on outings to the Yiddish theatre, perhaps, and ate *hamantashen* – which is a triangular pastry filled with poppy seed, raisins and honey.

Most people considered *Pesach* (Passover) the best festival of all and one which seemed to combine religion, tradition, family-gathering and caring for the less fortunate. Two to three weeks before the festival began, mother started scrubbing her home from top to bottom to get rid of any *chometz* – everything that is forbidden to eat, particularly products containing yeast – during the eight days of the festival. Young boys went round the streets with tin buckets

11

and hot coals offering to burn *chometz* for a small fee and house-wives sold their *chometz* to non-Jewish employees of the syna-gogue for a token sum. Fathers and children played their parts by sweeping up any stray crumbs with a feather and tray by candle-light the night before the *Seder* (the festive Passover meal). The Yiddishe Mama further prepared for this festival by lining her cupboards and dressers with fresh lining paper, stockpiling 120 or so white eggs – which were known as a 'long dozen' and of which only 100 were paid for – and boxes of *matzos* made by Bonns or, later, Manischewitz. She baked her *Pesach* specialities such as macaroons, almond biscuits and fluffy pancakes sprin-kled with sugar commonly called *boobeles* or *chemslers* and her children knew that this was the time of year when they had to abandon their nosh in the streets and look to mother's cooking for treats and goodies. If there was money to spare, mother bought her children new clothes that, more often than not, had to last them the year. The more observant in the community used special crockery, cutlery, pots and pans for the *Pesach* week alone and these could be bought for a few shillings from markets or shops such as Woolworths. Disputes sometimes arose over what was considered 'kosher for *Pesach*' and what was not and these were taken to the rabbi. A grocer's daughter remembered that her father could not sell cabbage or lettuce over *Pesach* because 'bugs were not kosher' and even non-Jewish grocers, such as Hawkins, on the corner of Commercial Road and New Road – opposite the Sussex Laundry – divided their shop up into two sections; one 'kosher for *Pesach*' and the other, not, because they were reluctant to miss out on valuable trade!

Worshippers in the community did not usually need to travel far to celebrate high days and holy days as there were sometimes as many as two or three synagogues on a street. Some were tiny and built onto or behind houses and others had beautifully furnished interiors. If members could not donate large sums of money for membership or maintenance of the buildings, they sometimes gave their workmanship instead and these gifts were labours of love. Men might build arks from beautifully carved oak and women sew curtains for the ark or dressings for the Torah and the reader's table.

4. Northwood Road Synagogue. When the synagogue was demolished, the art was saved and reconstructed at King Solomon High School, Barkingside. [Courtesy of King Solomon High School.]

It has to be said that life was not always wonderful. However Jewish you felt, you might still live in terrible poverty and the streets might still ring to the sound of the Yiddish curses and arguments which were the everyday language for some. Jewish humour, which is often self-deprecating, subtle, peppered with funny-sounding 'foreign' or Yiddish words and usually accompanied by extravagant hand gestures and facial contortions, offered a reprieve from hardship and it often seemed that the greater the difficulties, the more people depended on humour to survive. Only a Jew might find funny, for example, the story of the little girl who, when separated from her mother in Selfridges, told kindly attendants that her name was *bubbele tchoochele* (sweetie darling). The Yiddish Theatre provided another escape from poverty – even if only in fantasy – by frequently staging plays with a similar theme, that being the path from Russia and a life of poverty through improvement to America and inevitable wealth!

Whatever the living conditions, the community spirit was strong. Neighbours celebrated the births of each others' babies and rallied round with food and comfort when anyone passed away. Jewish people who fell on hard times or had never known good times could go to soup kitchens for the Jewish poor where they were provided with food. These visits were sources of shame, unfortunately, so were made only as a last resort. The most deprived in the community were given clothes and shoes by the Board of Guardians or the Jewish Free School. No Jewish child ever ran around bare-footed – the Yiddishe Mama ensured this. The East End Jews felt sufficiently confident as a group to band together to stop Oswald Moseley and his 'Blackshirts' from marching through the heart of their territory. Jews stood side by side with Communists and dockworkers to prevent the Fascists' forward march, and, in so doing, defied the Board of Deputies' entreaties for them simply to 'lock up their shops'. One of the consequences of this act of courage was that political uniforms were banned by Parliament.

Whether Orthodox or irreligious, rich or poor, all life – to a certain extent – was Jewish life. Your Jewish traditions defined you and shaped your days. Most members of our reminiscence groups recall their heritage with pride.

Schooldays

Mr Johnson Hammond Willis, teacher at Settle Street School held on to his waistcoat lapels and said, repeatedly, 'Remember the ant, thou sluggard, consider his ways and be wise!' Like his colleagues, Mr Rosenheim and Miss Barnet from Christian Street School, Mr Johnson Hammond Willis is remembered by his one-time pupils. Some regarded school as 'a source of colour in their lives' and others sang 'one more day and we shall be free at last from the house of misery' when their brief schooling careers drew to an end at the tender age of just 14.

Most East End children went to the school nearest to their homes. Even if this school was not a Jewish one, it was not uncommon to find that the majority of pupils in the schools were Jewish. Notwithstanding this, the first few weeks in English-speaking schools were often quite traumatic for children whose mother tongue was Yiddish. Boys usually wore hobnail boots to school, school caps and socks held up with elastic. Short trousers were *de rigueur* until bar mitzvah age when it was no longer considered to be 'unhealthy' for them to wear long trousers. Girls at primary level could wear what they liked. Many wore box-pleated drill slips with large navy knickers underneath. Handkerchiefs were sometimes concealed in pockets in knickers or pinned on jumpers to save the embarrassment of lifting up skirts every time girls needed to blow their noses. Older girls wore liberty bodices with suspenders attached to them and lyle stockings in winter.

15

Some children started all-day school at the early age of 3. These weary toddlers would lie down for afternoon naps on mattresses or inverted tables strung with hammocks provided for the purpose. As children progressed through the school system, it was quite the norm for them to find themselves in classes of up to 30 or 40. Classes were labelled one to seven and pupils in year seven were aged 14. In winter months, classrooms were heated only by coal fires, which warmed the teachers' backs but left some pupils numb with cold when the flames went out in the afternoons. Classroom desks were made of wood and were usually placed one behind the other in stepped rows. Each desk had an inkwell on it and some boys pushed the plaits of unsuspecting girls into these inkwells during moments of boredom. However, most pupils considered it an honour to be elected 'ink monitor.' Several people were sufficiently bright to have reached year seven at the young age of 11, but lack of parental support or teaching resources forced them to repeat the year until they reached the school leaving age of 14. Equally, students who made insufficient progress were kept down to repeat the year: most pupils found this process humiliating. Some children passed scholarship exams in arithmetic and 'composition' at the age of 11 and were fortunate enough to go on to Grammar or Central Schools. Those who failed – or could not afford the uniform – received no further education and many potential doctors, teachers or politicians became milliners, tailors, furriers or market traders in this way. A man told us that he was not allowed to attend school until the age of 12 because he was epileptic. The school pronounced him 'educated enough for his needs' at the age of 13 when he left to go into the family fishmongers. He never learned to read or write.

During the winter months there were double sessions at schools on Fridays. This meant that lunch hours were shortened and schools closed earlier to allow Jewish pupils to go home for *Shabbat*. Sick children received milk at schools and the poorest children often ate the food cooked in cookery lessons for their lunch. Doctors made recommendations for free milk or malt and London County Council (LCC) doctors visited schools regularly to ensure that these recommendations were implemented. It was not uncommon for over-protective mothers to stand by railings at break time handing food to their precious children, 'lest they starve.' A man told us that he took sandwiches to school every day. An older, stronger bully snatched them away from him explaining that his family was too poor to feed him. The younger child's mother wisely resolved the conflict by making sandwiches for both boys, who later became firm friends – notwithstanding the differences in age, size and, as it happened, religion.

Bullying was a common feature of school life and teachers did a great deal of the bullying. Children's personalities were sometimes subdued by fear – or from neglect – and thoughts of harsh treatment in schools remain in some memories well into old age. Each school formed its own policy on type and severity of punishment that was often inflicted with the intention of causing fear, humiliation or – worse – pain. Pupils' names were entered into 'punishment books' and wrong-doers might have to endure the embarrassment of standing in a corner wearing a dunce's cap or a sign, or staying in after school for half an hour to write lines. Caning was common – even for minor offences – and in some schools, such as Coburn Grammar School in Bow, girls received the same treatment as boys. Teachers sometimes threw chalk at pupils or rapped them over the knuckles or pulled their ears for offences as minor as blotting their copybooks. Enraged pupils rubbed orange peel on their hands to ease the pain after a caning and some boys put their caps down their trousers so that the beatings would not hurt as much. A man remembered being 'copped out' – that is to say, hit – on a regular basis merely because he could not paint, and teachers often bullied and ridiculed left-handed children for the simple reason that they could not 'write properly' with their right hands. These pupils were sometimes forced to do so – with disastrous consequences in later life. In one school any child caught talking in the classroom was forced to wear a sandwich board with the picture of a tongue pasted on it and to walk from classroom to classroom so that 'everybody could see what happened to a chatterbox.' Children who wore spectacles were teased but poverty sometimes prevented those in need from wearing them, anyway. Only the bravest parents complained to the school about their children's treatment but their English was seldom good enough for them to be effective. The more usual response of the immigrant parent was to smack the child at home for having misbehaved in school.

If a pupil played truant, the truant officer would pay a visit – albeit futile at times – to families where little English was spoken or understood. In some cases, parents were quite relieved not to be able to communicate, as they needed their children's help at home. A lady told us that she stayed away from school to help with housework every time her mother or younger siblings were ill. A man said that he had played truant for four months when a boy. He told his teacher that his father had died. As ill luck would have it, his teacher chanced to meet his father in the street. Both parent and teacher gave the boy a good hiding.

The dynamic between parents and teachers was often complicated. Teachers were not well paid – which fact may have accounted for their aggression. Parents suggested that teachers, at least, had a secure job and a pension – which was more than they could say for themselves. Most teachers were men; women gave up teaching on marriage. Some people remembered their teachers' shiny suits, which often smelled, needed cleaning and had leather patches on the elbows. Most parents were unable to help with homework, or even to sign forms. One man said that he had to guide his father's hand across a page in an attempt to help him write his name rather than leave his imprint in the shape of a cross!

Some good came out of the schooling system. There were outings and sports events and half-day holidays on public celebrations like Saint George's Day and Empire Day when every pupil sang patriotic songs and was made to salute the flag. Pupils learned to appreciate art, music and poetry; some learned the joy of reading. On school 'swimming days' teachers stood at the side of the pool and supported children in the water with sticks. Some Jewish mothers refused to allow their children into pools for fear of illness. No pupil showered after swimming so it was easy to identify the swimmers by the smell of chlorine. Boys learned carpentry and metalwork and girls, housewifery. At Villereal School in Thrawl Street, the older girls cleaned the staff room and brought in garments to iron as part of their lesson. Children's teeth were checked and their scalps examined for nits or lice by 'Nitty Nora' the school nurse.

5. A good reference was all-important for obtaining a job after leaving school. Hilda Buckner received this letter of recommendation from Virginia Road School, Bethnal Green.

There was no school-leaving ceremony and pupils left school as soon as they had turned 14. Pupils were simply given a slip of paper with the local labour exchange's address written on it. Some students received a leaving certificate as a reference. This was a mixed blessing, as the frequently featured phrases like 'this child was bad' or 'periodically late' or 'badly behaved' often acted as obstacles to future employment. There was no careers advice and

This is the job you want!

Due to increasing production, SIMPSON, the makers of the famous DAKS Clothes have immediate vacancies for women and girls, 15/35 years of age—skilled, semi-skilled, or unskilled. This is an opportunity you should grasp. Here in excellent conditions, you join a team of first-class workers making clothes of which they are proud.

Starting rates of pay:—
School Leavers. Girls at 15 years £3.10.0. Girls at 16 years £4.0.0.
Unskilled Women for training Full time 18 35 years £5.5.0.
There are also vacancies for Experienced Machinists, Handworkers etc
Excellent opportunities—permanent employment—highest rates of pay
for skilled workers.

Notice to Parents

School leavers are specially advised to take this opportunity to make a career. Training in machining and handwork is given by qualified instructors in the training school. Girls can learn a craft and a standard of workmanship that will stand them in good stead all their lives. Five-day week, Canteen, Sports and Social Club.

Apply at once to

Personnel Officer,
S. Simpson Limited,
92/100 Stoke Newington Rd., N.16
Tel. : CLIssold 1212

Trolleybuses 683, 643, 647, 649, 543
and Bus 76 all stop at factory.

6. Job advertisement for Simpson's, Stoke Newington Road. [Courtesy of the British Museum Newspaper Library, Colindale.]

jobs were at a premium. The lucky few found work in offices but most children worked with their families. Some children entered the sweatshops the week after they finished school. Letters of recommendation were required for entry to these sweatshops, which have repeatedly been described as 'unpleasant' and sometimes 'worse than even the worst of schooldays.' Whatever the benefits or scars, and wherever education led, life continued. At the very least, the acquisition of a better grasp of the English language integrated this immigrant population into the community at large.

The 'Front Room'

A 'front room' established your position in the neighbourhood; even if you did not own your property. This room – also called the sitting room, morning room, parlour (*die gute stube* or salon if you were of European extraction) – told the community that you had reached a certain level of economic stability and social status. Because the feeling of community was paramount, conformity of style reigned. One front room was very much like another – dark, cold, formal and tidy. However, this room was often shrouded in secrecy, its doors kept locked and the furniture covered with dust-sheets. This meant that families were often short of space. In the interests of maintaining one's social standing, however, this was an accepted sacrifice.

In the homes of the less fortunate, life centred on the black range in the kitchen. This was the cast iron cooker that also heated the kitchen and had to be cleaned with black lead. Because there weren't many possessions, large families could congregate in just two or three rooms and sometimes children slept 'top to tail' – four to six in one bed. Like the tide of social fortune, housing and interior design was a constantly changing agenda. Breadwinners often had seasonal work (such as in the garment industry) and lodgers had to be taken in during times of unemployment. In one family, the precious front room became the daughter's bedroom when times were hard. The lodger usurped the poor girl's bed. Another family's straitened circumstances drove the children to the *schlufbank*, which was pulled out of hiding to accommodate them at night. The children huddled together in the cold dreaming of owning pyjamas – the comfort of the middle classes! Front rooms were seldom heated and kitchens usually provided the houses' only warmth. In the older houses gas lamps lit the rooms. In more affluent households, gas mantles, which were delicate and broke easily, protected the flames.

When company arrived on high days and holy days, the front room's locked doors were thrown open with pride. On *Shabbat* families often dined here at a table that was covered with a white damask cloth or runner for the occasion in place of the usual chenille. There might be a green glass fruit bowl filled with fruit in the centre of the table, flanked by candlesticks that were usually made of brass, or silver – if you were lucky. Rag and bone men often gave green glass dishes in exchange for clothes – that is if they did not provide goldfish or lollipops for the children. Families would acquire sets of these dishes and display them among their ornaments. The silver candlesticks were sometimes displayed on trays during the week or wrapped up and hidden in wardrobes until it was appropriate to retrieve them. In desperate times, some families took their silver to pawnshops until *Shabbat*. By social convention, children waited to marry until the 'front room' had been furnished. Not only could parents then formally receive potential suitors, they could do so in style. A lady told a story of her first visit to her prospective mother-in-law's home. In her excitement she spilled tea on the shining damask cloth on the front room table. Mother-in-law replied in a heavy Yiddish accent: 'Never mind, dear, laundries also have to live!'

Front rooms were seldom re-decorated. Floorboards were draughty, often dirty and covered with rugs – if money permitted. Lino, which resembled parquet flooring, came into use later. The walls were usually brown or cream and mainly papered and the upholstery was burgundy or brown – particularly during the 1920s and 1930s – and dark red in the 1940s. Crocheted or linen antimacassars were draped over the backs of settees or the three-piece suites to protect them. Jewish families rarely introduced green into their decorative schemes as it was deemed unlucky. Those who could afford it used flocked wallpaper and a decorator to put it up.

Decorators were called 'paperhangers' and they usually slapped paper onto paper with glue made of flour and water. The build-up of paper on walls trapped bugs (*vanzen*) between the layers, and this was one of the reasons why so many houses were infested. In less affluent households, distemper was used when decorating or father hung the paper himself. A popular song at the time went 'When father papered the parlour, you couldn't see

7. Housing conditions in the East End were frequently poor. However, the tenants of Mr Hyman Cohen were probably unusual in taking direct – and successful – action. [Courtesy of Tower Hamlets Archive, Bancroft Road Library.]

him for paint...' Curtains ranged from heavy velvet drapes and/or thick cotton net to coloured paper (which resembled stained glass and was sometimes stuck to the windows) in place of fabric. Sometimes a curtain hung over the mantelpiece and rolled up newspaper – itself, upholstered at times – kept draughts from the windows at bay.

The centrepiece of the room was the piano, if you were very lucky. The piano was usually upright. Grand pianos graced the homes of the privileged few. Whatever the shape, if you had a piano you needed your neighbours to know this. One lady would call out emphatically to her children in the street 'I've left your sandwiches on the *piano*, children.' Remember that walls were very thin! Whether or not the piano was played or lessons could be afforded was another story.

8. A front room. [Courtesy of Lila Leigh.]

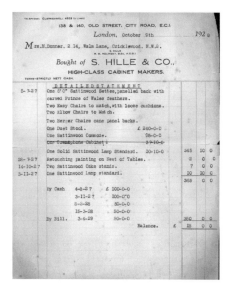

9. A bill from S. Hille & Co. for the front room above. [Courtesy of Lila Leigh.]

Aside from musical furniture, most of the rest of the furniture in the front room was conventional, often heavy, and chosen either by married couples or their parents. Cabinet making was a popular Jewish trade, so furniture was often homemade or made by friends. Otherwise, S. Hille & Co. (High-class Cabinet Maker of Old Street) and Epstein were two of the favoured furniture manufacturers for the more prosperous. Bills for furniture were paid in cash and by instalments, even by the more well to do.

Once householders had acquired the essential furniture and candlesticks, other ornaments followed on according to a scale reflecting social status. Chinese vases, dolls, china bulls and, later, flying ducks were popular choices. These might have been bought from Woolworth or acquired at outings to fairs. A three-tier cake stand made of china or a green glass fruit bowl filled with fruit was a particular sign of prosperity. One lady told the story of her family's china cows whose udders had to be clad in knickers in order to preserve propriety when company arrived. Poorer families were often too proud to display their ornaments and thus appear frivolous. 'Why spend your money on a flying duck when your family is short of eating the same?' Aspidistra plants, which lasted, were favoured. Their leaves were lovingly cleaned with cold tea or castor oil. For practical purposes, paper flowers were also popular choices. Fresh flowers were seldom displayed in this little-used room. Similarly, 'live interior design,' such as budgerigars in cages, was not deemed 'Jewish enough.' Some families who could not afford grandfather clocks displayed 'grandmother' clocks on their mantelpieces and family portraits or photographs were often hung on walls. Photographs of deceased loved ones superimposed on photographs of their tombstones were design features of the 1920s, and in the 1940s some front rooms boasted a 'peach mirror' that had flowers or crinolined ladies engraved onto the glass. By the 1940s most families had wind-up gramophones and radios in their front rooms, which became scenes of entertainment and sometimes dancing.

As time went on, social mores changed and Jewish communities were assimilated. Bright neon strips, which buzzed and caused headaches, replaced gas in the 1950s and 1960s, and fitted-carpet replaced floorboards. Women were gradually emancipated and status no longer depended so much on the state of your front room. But that is another story...

Going Steady

Every pot gets its cover – or so it was said. There was no one completely unmarriageable and the *shadchan* (matchmaker) could always be employed to redeem those incapable of helping themselves. The process of courtship was governed by ritual and the rather restrictive codes of conduct were broken only during the War years when dramatic changes and shifts in perspective took place. Jewish people 'went steady' or 'went serious' and the whole process might begin in Whitechapel High Street or Commercial Road, where boys and girls dressed in their finery would stroll up and down looking for talent – a ritual known as the 'Monkey Parade.' The end of the process – God willing – was marriage, of course; a most important event in the community.

Every family member played his/her part on the journey from introduction to consummation. Every girl's mother hoped for a wealthy son-in-law and every boy's mother, a 'suitable' girl. If the groom was not wealthy, at least let him be a butcher, a baker or fishmonger so that the daughter might never starve. Better still, a boy with a profession. Gamblers were bad news. Girls who would not listen married gamblers and lived 'to regret their decision.' Most of the time, despite their parents' machinations, children married into families that were equally poor. Younger siblings usually waited to see their older siblings married first as it was common for children to marry in chronological order. Youngest daughters could wait for some time if older daughters were in no hurry to tie the knot. Having said this, double standards in the community meant that girls were 'over the hill' if they remained unmarried at 24. Boys, however, escaped this fate.

It was acceptable for some girls to work – unpaid – for their fathers after marriage, but it was not usually acceptable for women to have careers until the War years and, for most, marriage was the only option. There was no excuse not to find a husband and the quest for one was serious business. People such as Mr Stern, who doubled as a fruit seller in Brick Lane, made good money making *shidduchs* (matches). The uglier the girl, the bigger the fee! We heard the story of a wealthy 'old' spinster of 30 who was introduced by a matchmaker to a poor 17-year-old student. They married, had eight children, and the husband pre-deceased his wife. Did anyone ask if they were happy? Of course not. Everyone said, 'Thank God, thank God. At least they are married with children.' Some of the more questioning in the community regretted the loss of freedom and independence that marriage brought – 'like an enema to a dead body!' as the saying went.

Yiddish newspapers carried advertisements for prospective sons-in-law with promises of shares in the family business for suitable applicants. The most important question asked of such candidates was *Kann er macht ein leben?* – 'Can he make a living?' If the boy answered in the affirmative and was Jewish to boot, cries of 'Thank God, he's not a goy, thank God she's got a boy!' would be heard all round. Girls were required to be virgins as well as Jewish and there were hierarchies here too. *Chuts* (Dutch Jews), were scorned by Russian Jews for being too anglicised; and *Polacks* (Polish Jews), scorned by *Litvacks* (Lithuanians) for being less educated. A girl's good reputation was paramount and a girl was always advised to 'be good' on a date. No one wanted to be called a flirt (worse still, a *flak* or tart) who 'went much further.' Ironically enough, the social freedom that came with the otherwise restricted war years, put paid to a lot of this prejudice and superstition. People moved out of tight-knit communities and social fencing-in to the wider community where they were Jews in a secular world. Morals were loosened and rules re-learned. Respect for soldiers meant that beer was often served to them free of charge. This resulted in a more confident approach to women. Equally, Jewish fiancés were often dumped when some young girls discovered the 'fun' to be had with visiting GIs. It is not surprising, therefore, that some people considered the War years 'the best of their lives.'

Prior to the War, holding hands or a good night kiss was as far as it went if the young man was respectable and his intentions good. Kissing was not a particularly 'English' custom. As the song went, 'A kiss on the cheek is quite continental...' The families of married couples-to-be shook hands on first meeting and, once married, a young girl never kissed her mother-in-law except, perhaps, on *Shabbat* after the candles had been lit. A man told us that his youth club organised rambling sessions on Saturdays. Because there were surreptitious 'kissing sessions' after the rambling, the club was inundated with requests to join!

It was not easy for courting couples to find privacy. The back row of the cinema was cosy, but cost money. Otherwise, youngsters would find themselves sitting with parents who showed no inclination to budge. A lady told us that while she succeeded – after some effort – in dislodging her mother, the latter called out 'Don't forget to bring up the *gezunder* (chamber pot)' on her way up to bed. There was no sex education so young men sought the advice of their older peers in secret places in playgrounds or on the streets. They might then attempt to put theory into practice behind the sheds in Victoria Park. Few girls in the community were willing to risk the shame of an unwanted pregnancy and for those unfortunate enough to become pregnant, a rushed wedding was the only choice.

Once an understanding was reached, young couples might go to shops such as Feldmans or Fishbergs in Black Lion Yard, Weingarten in Aldgate, Inwalds or Jack Robinson, Wholesalers for their engagement ring. The two families usually met for afternoon tea which was served from the best china 'without chips' in the front room. The girl's parents always provided a *nudden* (dowry) that might be purchased from Wickhams in Mile End or Stephens in Stoke Newington and paid for 'on the never-never.' The dowry

10. A receipt for a wedding ring from H. Fifer Jeweller in Paget Road. The stamps (for 2d) represent the tax payable on the ring.

usually included linen the mother had bought with her from the *heim*. The bride's parents also paid for the wedding – despite the not infrequent protestations made by the groom's parents that their plans weren't lavish enough for their son. A secret concern, sometimes voiced, was that any rich girl would have fallen for their son – even though he was a humble tailor. Equally, the girls' parents worried particularly about whether prospective sons-in-law gambled, or drank, or were able to support the daughter as they would wish. One man remembered having to sell his business in the 1930s to pay for his daughter's wedding. Another told us that his parents-in-law could not afford to pay for the caterer so his parents, who found themselves in the same position, gave an assurance that a wealthy uncle's wedding gift of money would foot the bill. At the last minute, the uncle decided to give the young couple 12 silver fish knives and 12 silver fish forks instead. The caterer was 'knocked' – that is to say, he remained unpaid. There was no money for him and what was he to do with fish forks? Some young couples paid for their own weddings with money given to them as presents. Two guineas was the average amount given before the War and it was always given in cash. Some of the more unscrupulous guests waited to see whether the food and seating arrangements at the reception were to their liking before deciding on the size of their gift!

OSTWIND & CO.

Bakers, Pastrycooks & Restaurateurs.

Bride and Birthday
Cake Specialists.

Branch:
56, Golders Green Rd,
London, N.W.11,
Phone: SPEedwell 0062.

Head Office:
75/9 Wentworth Street,
E.1.
Phone: Bishopsgate 6858.

CONTRACT.

Made this *16th* day of *July 1942* between Messrs. Ostwind & Co. Caterers of 75 Wentworth Street, E.1. and *Mr Weiss 15 West Bank N16* for the catering of a wedding reception to be held on *Oct 25th* at *Marcus Samuel Hall* between the hours of: *2 PM & 5.30 P.M*

The Caterers will provide:
Snack Bar consisting of various assorted cocktail dainties and appetisers, salted nuts, chocolates and sweets.

Reception consisting of:
Tea, Coffee, Minerals, Still Drinks.
Assorted Sandwiches, Bridge Rolls (Smoked Salmon, Anchovy, Egg & Cress, Sardines, Lettuce, Tomato, Cucumber, Cream Cheese and Olive, Asparagus Tips, etc)
Various Dainty Cakes, Biscuits and Pastries.
Cream Gateaux.   Fruit Salad and Cream.   *Trifles & Cream*

The Caterers will also provide all the necessary utensils, tables, linen, china, glassware, cutlery, table and floral decorations, menus and a full and efficient staff.
The Caterers will also provide, if required,
(a) The Cakes for the Bride House, at an extra charge of £1.   *To be*
(b) A Band of   musicians @ 30/- each.   *decided*
(c) Barman at an additional charge of £1.10.0.   *later.*

The price that is to be paid to the caterers for the above is:
11/3 per guest for a guaranteed minimum of *120* guests, additional guests to be charged proper. *10/-*
In witness whereof the two parties to this contract have hereunder set their hands.

Deposit £4

P.p. OSTWIND & CO.

11. A bill for the catering of a wedding reception.

WEDDING DRINK BILL.

◆

FATHER WHO EXPECTED "OTHER SIDE" TO PAY.

An unpaid bill for wines and spirits for a wedding feast led to proceedings at Shoreditch County Court yesterday by Mr. Elias Frumkin, a wine merchant, of 162 Commercial-road, E., against Mr. N. Simons, a bookmaker's clerk, and his wife, D. Simons, of 21 Colberg-place, Stamford Hill, for £16 17s. 4d. (debt and costs).

Mr. S. M. Fruitman, solicitor representing the judgment creditor, told Judge Lilley that judgment was obtained against defendants in the Whitechapel Court on May 26th last for £14 1s. and costs, the debt being the balance of an account for £33 for wines and spirits for the wedding feast of defendants' daughter at the First Avenue Hotel, Holborn, in January last. Payment under the judgment was to be made "forthwith."

The male defendant appeared and, in reply to Mr. Fruitman, said that as a bookmaker's clerk he was paid sometimes £2 10s. a week and sometimes £3. If his employer had a good week he sometimes paid him a bit extra. The betting was at "The dogs."

His Honour: Who ordered these goods?

Mr. Simons: My wife.

Were your means the same as now? —Yes.

Then how did you expect to pay?—I was given to understand that the goods would be paid for by "the other side," but they were not.

An order was made for the payment of £3 a month.

WEDDING GUESTS ROBBED

◆

Fur Coats Stolen At Synagogue

Twelve fur coats, valued at about £5,000, were stolen on Sunday evening whilst a wedding reception was in progress at the New Synagogue, Egerton-road, Stamford Hill. The robbery was carried out in under 10 minutes.

The wedding was that of Miss Lilian Miller, aged 25, of 31 Ravensdale-road, Stamford Hill, to Mr. Benjamin Mason, a 35-years-old optician, who lives at Hendon.

CHOSE ONLY THE BEST

The theft was discovered when Mr. W. M. Kurwen, of Park-lane, W., went to the cloakroom to get his wife's mink coat, said to be worth £3,000. He called the caretaker's wife because the door was locked, but her key would not open it, the inside latch having been put up. The door was broken open.

There were more than 20 fur coats in the cloakroom, but the thieves had chosen only the 12 best.

An elderly lady who was looking after a child in the next room did not hear a sound.

13. *Hackney Gazette*, 1948.

12. Not all bills were settled amicably. *Hackney Gazette and North London Advertiser*, 2 July 1937.

During the 1930s the bride always wore a white dress, which was often made by a local dressmaker for very little money. The wealthy few went to specialist shops such as Jean Conn in Bond Street 'to copy the Duchess of Windsor's wedding dress.' Beaded or sequined gowns were all sewn by hand. During the War, brides often borrowed dresses or were married in suits. Rationing meant

An Interrupted Honeymoon

◆

POULTERER'S STORY OF A WEDDING GIFT

Charges against two poulterers—Harry Kaye, 31, of Stamford-grove, Stamford Hill, and Norman Kerstein, 28, of 88 Kyverdale-road, Upper Clapton—of receiving 64 eggs, two cartons of butter, and three pints of milk, were withdrawn at the North London Magistrates' Court on Thursday, and the police proceeded on charges under the rationing regulations.

There were pleas of not guilty.

It transpired that the food was found in a van driven by Kaye, with Kerstein as a passenger, which was stopped by the police at half-past 11 at night.

EGGS LAID ON THE JOURNEY

Detective-sergeant Lusty stated that when they first appeared in Court he told the accused there would have to be a remand for inquiries to be made, and Kaye said: "You won't be able to make many inquiries about the eggs. They were laid by the chickens during the journey." (Their van was laden with cases of chickens).

Kaye, giving evidence said he was married on the Sunday before they were stopped, and, because of the "go-slow" on the railway, had to interrupt his honeymoon to go to Hereford market and collect a load of poultry. A farmer friend of his, Mr. Hill, gave him the food as a wedding present.

Questioned by Detective-sergeant Lusty, witness said his friend had about 1,000 chickens. He did not often give butter away.

14. There were always ways of getting around rationing.
Hackney Gazette, 16 December 1946.

that no one wanted to waste valuable clothing coupons on a wedding dress. Bridegrooms wore morning suits often hired from Young's in Wardour Street, Losners in Brick Lane and Stamford

Hill and Moss Bros in Covent Garden for the *chupah* (wedding canopy), and usually changed into white tie and tails for the evening. Female guests usually wore suits or day frocks for the *chupah* then changed into evening dresses for the celebration party.

The bride would leave her home – right foot first for luck – and be whisked off to the service in a waiting car. Cars – which were usually paid for by the groom's parents – were sent off to gather all the immediate family to the synagogue. As families were large, neglected members frequently took offence and caused a *broigus* (quarrel). 'If you forgot – or were forgotten – God help you!'

Waiting cars usually took the bridal couple to a photographer's studio after the ceremony. Suss, a popular photographer in the 1920s, often sat the bride on a chair before her groom – a ploy particularly favoured by men of smaller stature than their chosen women. Boris took over from Suss in the 1930s and might have owed his success to the fact that he touched up his photographs to eliminate the bride's blemishes: 'all Boris's brides looked beautiful.' Boris stood the groom on a block draped with material, in front of a Hollywood-style backdrop. Henry Shaw was the favoured photographer of the late 1930s and 1940s. Once the photographs had been taken, the partying began. La Boheme was a 'very posh' venue, favoured by a privileged few. Stern's Hotel, King's Hall opposite the Grand Palais, and a hall in Tottenham called 'Salo e Belle' were also popular. In desperate times, the wedding party might be held in the factory or workroom, especially cleared and cleaned for the purpose. Monnickendams, Goides, Shaverein and Bonn in Aldgate were among the most popular caterers. Whisky, brandy and cherry brandy were usually served at the table and wine merchants might do a deal for whisky at 11s 3d a bottle rather than 12s 6d a bottle so that families might order their wine directly from them. Beer was never served. Food was much higher on the agenda than drink, and there were always guests who claimed to have 'eaten themselves unconscious!' At the end of the wedding party, the cook would position herself by the door in expectation of tips and waitresses would ask guests for money after dinner had been served. Waitresses at children's tables often drew the short straw and children were sent to ask their parents for money.

Few could afford the luxury of a honeymoon. A night at the Cumberland Hotel or a week in Blackpool or Southend sufficed.

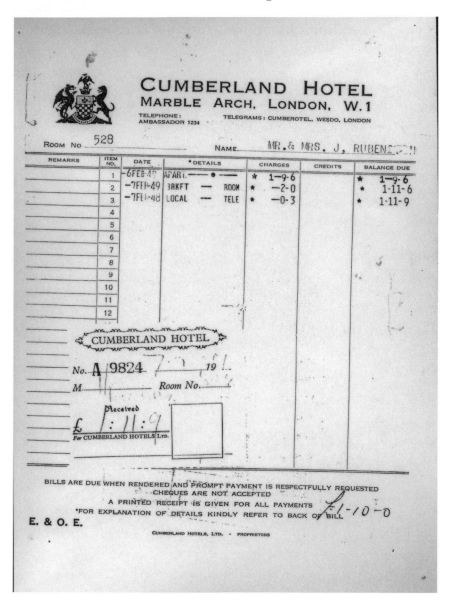

15. Whom did Anne Rubin phone on her honeymoon night? Her mother, of course!

The more well to do might choose one of the many Jewish guest-houses or hotels in Bournemouth or Brighton.

On the whole, everyone in both families and the community at large returned home from the celebrations satisfied. Parents could then turn their focus on the next sibling in the line for whom – God willing – the whole process might begin again.

Keeping Clean

Keeping clean without the luxury of a bathroom or inside lavatory was not easy. A community sprang up round this challenge with social mores all of its own. The few lucky enough to have a bathroom bathed infrequently in unheated bathrooms and those who were less fortunate bathed in a *vanna* (zinc bath), placed either in the kitchen or near the living room fire. Children were washed in chronological order – in the same water – beginning with the eldest. The last child to be bathed, endured water that was cold and dirty. Boys bathed separately from girls.

The majority of the adult community paid weekly visits to the baths. Most areas had at least one bathhouse and Thursday night or Friday afternoon visits became part of the weekly social ritual. There were public baths and private baths. Public baths were busy and lengthy queues formed for these; especially on Fridays. They were less expensive than private baths, costing as little as 3d a visit. Goulston Street public baths near Petticoat Lane were among the most popular. There was a swimming pool on the premises, too. If you had immersed yourself in the pool, a bath was not considered necessary as the chlorine dissolved the dirt. There were public baths in Commercial Road, Marshall Street and Oxford Street, among others. The Imperial in Russell Square was private and offered vapour baths. The private baths in both Poplar and Canon Street provided foam baths where you could soak at your leisure in 'soap up to your neck.'

Each public bathhouse contained about 40–50 baths, each placed in small cubicles. Men and women bathed at different times and it was generally considered appropriate for children to start using the baths after the age of 13. Soap and towels were provided, but the towels were much smaller than those provided in private baths. In fact, they 'hardly covered your privates,' appeared to be made out of 'dirty grey sandpaper,' and 'were not very good at getting you dry.' Although some people invested in their own soap – Lifeguard, Sunlight, Palmolive and transparent Pears being popular choices – for the majority of the bathing public, soap meant carbolic soap. During the War, when soap was scarce, small remnants of soap were heated in muslin and squeezed and recycled into bigger bars. It was difficult to maintain standards of hygiene in the army. One man told of putting a candle up and down the seam of his shirt to hear the crackling of the fleas! Special mobile shower units were set up for the purpose of delousing. Soda crystals, which were not perfumed until after the War, were often used to soften bath water. Deodorants were not much known before the War and dress pads were used to conceal and absorb sweat. Johnson's baby powder, Yardley's lavender water, or 'Tweed' by Lentheric, were smothered on to keep unpleasant smells at bay.

Bath attendants belonged to a special breed, and best behaviour was required in their presence. One of them was known as 'the Bath House Beast.' They controlled the water flow in the cubicles from outside panels. If the water was not sufficiently hot, the occupants might call out 'hot water number 5,' or 'Governor, hot water in number 26, please,' and hot water would gush through the taps. Needless to say, the system was not without its loopholes and the more mischievous might call out for cold water in another bath – with unpleasant consequences for the unsuspecting bather. If the attendants were displeased – or if the allocated time of about half an hour was up – they would bang on cubicle doors or simply drain out the bath water. Beyond their control, however, and despite the fact that they cleaned each bath after use, were the all-pervasive smells of sweat, damp and chlorine.

People chatted to each other over the cubicles: 'What are Millwall's chances in the Cup this year?,' 'Have you heard the latest…?' When their time was up, they emerged from bathing, 'bright, shiny and clutching a soggy towel.'

A steam bath or *schwitz* was the last word in luxury. Schevzik's in Brick Lane was the best known. Tuesday was ladies' day and, for the rest of the week, men bathed and were treated to massages or beatings with beech leaves or besoms. Clients sometimes

16. Schevzik's in Brick Lane were Russian Vapour Baths where men went to *schwitz* (sweat). Tuesday was ladies' day. [Courtesy of Tower Hamlets Archive, Bancroft Road Library.]

41

brought food in with them – 'half a chicken was nice' – or played cards away from their wives' prying eyes. Some men even settled in there for the night.

Men also enjoyed the luxury of weekly or fortnightly visits to the barbershop for hot towels on the face, a shave with a cutthroat razor and a 'short back and sides.' Some men left their named shaving cups and brushes at the barbershops, which were also the places to read girlie magazines and acquire contraceptives – 'something for the weekend, sir?' Barbershops were open until late at night and barbers worked long hours for little pay. Tips of one or two pennies were the norm. Apprentices – or 'lather boys' – worked for so little pay that they had to rely on tips. Those training to shave customers, practised with cutthroat razors on balloons until they were sufficiently skilled not to burst them. Pershana Aftershave, Vaseline Hair Tonic and Pomade Brilliantine were used by the fashionable, and some men became known as the 'patent leather kids' because they had shiny hair like Valentino, the heartthrob, or George Raft, the film star. Jars of Brylcreem were bought at the chemist's for four and a half pennies each. Brylcreem was very popular and it was hoped that – as the advertisement promised – it would keep you 'right on top.' It wreaked havoc with upholstery, however, and was one of the reasons why antimacassars were placed on chair backs. Any woman who ran her fingers through a man's hair had to expect a handful of grease!

Women used Californian Poppy Cream Perfume on their hair to smell good. They washed their hair with Armami or Drene shampoos; or, if desperate, chose between egg yolk, beer, teabags or vinegar. Friday night was shampoo night – 'Armami night' as the advertisement said. Hair was not usually washed in the baths because there were no dryers there and it was considered inadvisable to go outside with wet hair for fear of catching a chill. More to the point, there wasn't sufficient running water available to rinse out the soap or shampoo. Water used for hair washing at home was poured from a jug over the head and into a bowl. Hair was then vigorously towel rubbed or placed near a fire to dry – 'sometimes, too near!' Children had their hair combed with nit combs or doused with vinegar against nits. Nits and, worse still, lice were the dread of most children. If 'Nitty Nora' the school nurse, found a child with nits, she sent them to be cleansed at a cleansing station where a foul smelling lotion was poured over their heads. The shame of this was that everyone else could detect the culprit from his/her unusual smell. Children at Norwood Childcare Homes were sheared to the scalp on arrival as a precaution against nits. The result of this was that the boys and girls always looked alike.

17. Two young boys shaved clean to the scalp either to cure or prevent nits.

For the women, the more daring and modern might colour their hair at home. Hilton hair colour was used for blondes and Egyptian Henna turned the hair red. However, ladies' hair fashion was really only for the wealthy. Many women and girls never had haircuts and hair buns and plaits persisted for years. You risked being called a *kurve* (loose woman) if you dared to cut your hair in a 'bob' style. Some families cut their children's hair themselves. The pudding basin cut was so called because a basin was placed over the head and the hair was cut round it. The lucky few with barbers as relatives, visited them for haircuts.

In the 1940s, Housing Associations like the Guinness Trust began to put baths into flats, albeit in kitchens, where baths doubled up as tables by being covered with wooden boards, or oilcloths called *serratas*, when not in use. Like the *vannas* used before them, these baths were filled with water from the copper on the range. However, one could now empty them by pulling out the bath plugs. From the point of view of hygiene and ease of manoeuvre, progress was being made. However, many people mourned the loss of the friendship and unity that regular communal bathing brought and, in some ways, the gains of luxury and privacy dented the strength of the community.

Home Remedies

Superstitions, rituals and cures attending health and ill health circulated among the community between the Wars. There was no National Health Service, and doctors were expensive and often a last resort. Some of their medicines were considered less effective than favourite home cures. The mission doctor gave his services free of charge – but one paid in prayers: no treatment was given until the patient had attended a sermon and prayed – dripping blood on the floor notwithstanding! If medicine failed, there was mysticism. Charms such as a hand, which is a symbol of good luck, the Star of David, or a red ribbon, were worn as protection against the 'evil eye.' It was deemed unlucky to speak of good fortune – whether in the family or in business. Better to complain so as not to be cursed; but, if it came to it, cursed you were and with passion: 'May no evil eye avoid you,' 'May my enemies suffer like this,' 'May you become swollen and veined like a mountain,' 'May you burst from pleasure,' or 'Salt your eyes and pepper your nose.' If in error you let a compliment slip or praised a child's beauty, you spat three times as insurance against ill luck.

A sick baby might have his name changed to avert the Angel of Death; earth was placed in a protective circle around an ailing person's bed. If none of this worked it was because none of the good luck charms had been worn. In this climate of fear the 'home remedy' industry flourished. There was a cure for most ills – and none were too troublesome or preposterous.

Fat People

find no styles to fit

Excess fat is out of fashion. One can see that everywhere. Beauty, health and fitness demand its removal. And millions do remove it. Obesity is not one-tenth so common as it was.

That easy and pleasant way to reduce weight is with Marmola Prescription Tablets. Just take four a day. No abnormal exercise or diet is required.

The reduction is gradual, rarely exceeding a pound a day. So the body adjusts itself to the new condition.

Marmola has been used for 19 years. Countless people everywhere have learned its efficiency. They have told others, and the use has spread, until people now are taking 100,000 boxes monthly.

You can see in every circle what Marmola has done for your friends. Now learn what it means to you.

Our book tells you every ingredient, tells you just how it acts. You will know the reason for every good effect. Your own chemist will sign our guarantee.

This is the modern, scientific way to gain the slenderness you seek. Investigate it, test it now.

Marmola Prescription Tablets are sold by all chemists at 3/- per box, or sent post paid on receipt of price by the Marmola Co., 86, Clerkenwell Road, London, E.C. 1. Send this coupon for our latest book, a two-day sample free and our guarantee.

The Pleasant Way to Reduce

18. Patent medicines were popular for many ailments; and the fad for 'slimming' pills has a long history. [Courtesy of the British Museum Newspaper Library, Colindale.]

For example, here was a cure for sore throats. Take a sock hot off the foot. Fill the sock with salt that has just been heated on a tin plate. Place the sock around the neck and go to sleep. Wake up in the morning – cured! If, by chance, this fails, you could gargle with hot salt water – the more vile-tasting and nauseating the better; or have sulphur powder blown through paper at your tonsils. Pharmacists recommended painting sore throats or ulcerated mouths with Gentian Violet, which, as it's name suggests, coloured everything purple.

Headaches, backaches, or stomach aches were attributed to constipation, the diagnosing and curing of which spawned a home industry all of its own. Popular treatments included senna pods, which were soaked overnight, then strained, and the liquid drunk in the morning; others were liquid paraffin, Exlax, Syrup of Figs and Epsom Salts. Whether appropriate or not, Friday was the day for a dosing so that results could be felt at leisure on Saturdays. One lady remembered buying a black draught from a pharmacist as a constipation cure, and a man who had been in the army remembered 'Number 9' pills – so called because they proved their effectiveness nine times over! In extreme cases, soap was used as a suppository. If the diagnosis was not constipation, it might be indigestion, a common ailment in a culture of stodgy diets. The favoured cures for this were Milk of Magnesia or Globus Salts, the trade name for sodium sulphate. If backaches were not caused by constipation – and treated accordingly – small glass bulbs (sometimes filled with leeches or flaming surgical spirit) were placed strategically on areas of pain. These same glass bulbs (called *bunkus*) might just be heated and placed over the back as a cure for bronchitis. Miraculously no skin was ever burned!

Frequent colds were an everyday hazard with no easy cure. There were head colds, chest colds, stomach colds and bladder colds. The best cure for these was the Jewish 'penicillin': a bowl of home-made chicken soup. 'Feed a cold and starve a fever.' Otherwise one could choose between the options of the juice of a cooked onion, hot milk and honey, warm beetroot juice mixed with brown sugar or a camphor block hung round the neck. The smell of camphor or Vick Rub permeated a society where town smoke and smog made breathing hazardous. One of life's ironies was that shared sleeping accommodation provided warmth and comfort to those who were ill. There was little choice in this matter, however, and sleeping *kopf zu fuss* (head to foot) was a reality accepted by most. If there were *vanzen* in the beds, a home remedy was to take two grains of quick silver mixed with the whites of two eggs beaten together until frothy and to apply this with a feather to holes and crevices in the bedstead. However, the so-called 'red brigade' was always a threat to a good night's sleep. Someone remembered lying awake counting the bedbugs as they crawled up his walls: as the saying went, *tanzen mit vanzen* (dancing with bedbugs)! Local councils would come round to fumigate infested rooms, which were then sealed off for 24 hours before they could be entered again.

When children had whooping cough or croup, they were taken to road works to breathe in fumes from heated tar. Visits to the water near the Woolwich Ferry to breathe in fresh, so-called 'spa' air were also curative. Friars Balsam – although effective – proved less dramatic. Earaches were treated with heated olive oil poured down the ear and kept in place with cotton wool or a conspicuous headscarf. This cure was deemed so effective that painkillers were seldom used or doctors consulted.

Most poignant, perhaps, were home 'treatments' that required the community's support as a whole. When people suffered 'with their nerves' or were 'queer,' 'difficult,' or 'delicate' the community rallied round with tea, sympathy and guesses as to the probable cause. When you were down, you were down, and you were removed from the community only if you endangered it, when the lady from the Colney Hatch Mental Hospital might 'pay a visit.' Wincarnis, which was bought from grocer shops, was a popular tonic for 'nerves.' Although non-alcoholic, it was known as 'fortified wine' and was quite pleasant to drink. Most of the time, people 'got on with it' in the way they and their families had done before.

Someone told us the story of his sister's attacks of fright. A soothsayer in the community suggested she pour liquid under her bed before retiring for the night. In the morning the liquid had formed into the shape of a dog. A dog must have been the cause of her fear! Infant mortality and early deaths were everyday occurrences. The neighbours gathered together with food, offers of childcare and words of sympathy.

Women's problems were in a league of their own – and not always sympathetically treated. Dr Williams' pink pills or aspirin were prescribed for 'the monthly' although a stone hot water bottle heated up in a saucepan on the range was equally effective. A first period was rewarded with a slap so that blood would surge to another part of the body.

Chilblains were regarded as a necessary part of winter. These were caused by a combination of chilly homes and workplaces and close proximity to fires or single bar heaters. Most women rubbed their mottled legs with raw onion or garlic in the hope of a cure – but nothing really helped.

Rheumatism – now usually called arthritis – was a common affliction. Many women silently suffered with fingers disfigured from hand washing and floor scrubbing in freezing houses. Sloanes Liniment was rubbed into aching joints and buses often smelled of Winter Green Rub, which elderly ladies applied with thermogene pink wool pads by way of easing their pain.

Boils, which were a feature of everyday life, were often lanced with a cutthroat razor; whereas Fuller's Yeast was an effective cure for spots. Sties on the eye were treated with boracic crystals dissolved in distilled or boiled water, or with Golden Eye Ointment, a cure-all for most eye ailments. Cuts and grazes had iodine painted on them or – more ingeniously – spiders' webs placed round them to expedite healing. Horse 'shit' was placed on swollen knees! If you were merely 'off colour' you took Carters little liver pills. Nosebleeds were stemmed by dropping or placing a key, or ice, down the back, or merely by pinching the bridge of the nose.

Few people could afford to visit the dentist so teeth were cleaned by rubbing salt into them. If you had to pay a visit for an extraction, you usually drank whisky or brandy beforehand to deaden

---

WHERE NATURE . FAILS,
ART STEPS IN. .

ARTIFICIAL TEETH and

EXTRACTIONS.

23 Clapton Square & 11 Clapton Passage, N.E.

(Facing Round Chapel.)

PHONE, DALSTON 2005.

Hours of Attendance—10 a.m. to 10 p.m.

325: Lea Bridge Road, Markhouse Corner.
Queen's Road, Buckhurst Hill, Essex.

(Near Station.)

PHONE, WALTHAMSTOW 616.

Hours of Attendance—10 a.m. to 7 p.m.

HOWARD BENNETT, Principal.

---

19. A visit to a real dentist was a 'luxury' that few East Enders could afford. *Hackney Official Guide*, c. 1915. [Courtesy of Melbyn Brooks.]

the pain. For sixpence your teeth could be pulled in the market at a stall next to the brass band whose cacophony drowned the sound of the screams! A lady told us that she sat in dentists' or doctors' waiting rooms hoping that her patience might be rewarded by a sudden recovery prior to the consultation. Patients had to be patient and relationships with the caring professions were complicated.

There were several remedies for headaches, from vinegar and brown paper – as in the nursery rhyme – to raw potato skins; although it wasn't clear whether the skins themselves or lying down with them affected the cure.

In time, remedies became more sophisticated and community dynamics changed. However, in this resilient and hard-working group, much healing was achieved. Some of their home cures are acknowledged and practised to this day.

And So To Bed

Alf made a bedroom suite with a very large bed for his new wife. The bed was made in two parts. As he took it into his house, someone stopped and offered him a good price for the bed. He sold it. Business is business. Because his wife complained, he made her another identical bed, but it never stood up to the original. As far as she was concerned, no other bed would do. This was an inauspicious start to their marriage – whatever the profit gained!

Most of the community had brass or iron bedsteads that had metal springs and removable brass knobs. *Vanzen* – the plague of the times – could hide in these knobs and work their way into the bedding. Keatings Powder, a disinfectant, was liberally sprinkled over mattresses and into the hollows of the metalwork. Special spanners were used to tighten the screws that held the bed's framework secure, but the so-called 'red-brigade' were most persistent

20. For those whose rooms and beds were *tanzen mit vanzen* Keating's Powder provided one – temporary! – solution, 1939. [Courtesy of the British Museum Newspaper Library, Colindale.]

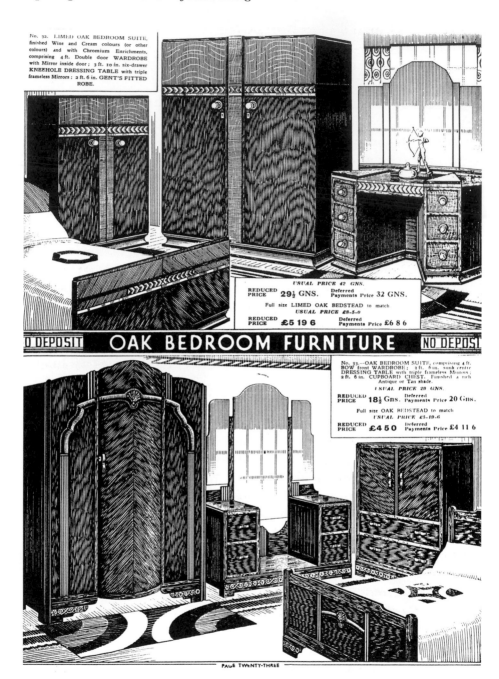

21. From the British Home and Colonial Furniture Stores catalogue, showing the wardrobes, dressing tables and chests that were in style during the 1930s. [Courtesy of Bruce Cohen, Group Managing Director and Chief Executive of Courts plc.]

bedfellows. A man told us how he took a candle to the bedbugs to burn them as they crawled up his walls in order to congregate on the picture rails. Alas, this was all to little avail!

As social and economic progress was made, beds might then be made of solid woods like maple or walnut. These beds were heavy and difficult to move. Pity one Benjy Cokeman (born Cohen), who, with his horse and cart, lugged furniture round the community. He was replaced by Pickfords, which hauled heavy furniture through windows with a crane. Some beds had elaborately carved and hand-dovetailed headboards. Matching twin wardrobes (one for male and one for female requirements), side tables, a cheval mirror, dressing table and washstand sometimes completed the set. The room might also be furnished with a tallboy (which is a tall drawer unit used to store linen), wicker rocking chairs, or basket chairs. Most desirable and upmarket was birdseye maple or mahogany furniture; better still, mahogany furniture inlaid with ivory. Because cabinet making was such a popular profession in the community, much of this furniture was often family-made.

If you didn't have a pot cupboard for storage – and pot cupboards might also be used to store medicines – you kept your *gezunder* or 'potty pic' (chamber pot) under the bed. The task of emptying the chamber pot fell to an unlucky family member. This, however, was a welcome alternative to dressing in coats and boots and trudging down icy paths to unlit and unheated outside lavatories. Boys sometimes urinated through open windows into their back yards, leaving their guilty imprint in the form of icy puddles that their parents or siblings found in the morning! Beds were built fairly high off the ground at the time and could conceal things aside from the *gezunder*. A man told us the story of the space under his parents' double bed that became his favourite hiding place when he was in trouble. Someone else spoke of the homemade wine which her parents kept under their bed and which spilled and filled the house with its smell every time her mother swept there.

Stone hot water bottles provided heat and sometimes even bricks that had been heated in the fire and wrapped in cloths warmed the beds. If the bedroom had a fireplace at all, it was usually lit

Elegant Ease...

Well-tailored pure silk pyjama with adaptable
neck-line, in a variety of multi-coloured stripes.

Bust 36 ins.   £8 . 14 . 11

Bust 38 ins.   £8 . 19 . 9

8 coupons.

JENNERS
PRINCES STREET EDINBURGH
LIMITED

22. Proper pyjamas and nightdresses were only affordable by the better off. These pure silk pyjamas would have been an unheard-of luxury for most people. *The Queen*, 5 May 1943. [Courtesy of the British Museum Newspaper Library, Colindale.]

only if a family member became ill. One family brought a shovel of burning embers from the front room fire to warm the bedroom. In the winter there was often a thick frost, affectionately known as 'Jack Frost', on the insides of the windowpanes. These were often stuffed with rolled-up newspapers to keep draughts at bay. Heavy cotton net curtains hung at almost every window, and if there were side curtains they were often made of remnants bought from market stalls.

Most bedrooms were lit by gas mantles, which provided more or less light at the turn of a knob. Gas mantles in the hall were sometimes left on low so that latecomers could turn them up before mounting the stairs. Candles were frequently used, especially in bedrooms and for visits to outside lavatories. Come bedtime, you snuggled into bed wearing your underwear or flannelette nightdress if you were a girl, and *gutkas* (combinations) if you were a boy. Only the better off possessed proper pairs of pyjamas, dressing gowns and slippers: after all, 'there were enough problems finding money for daytime clothes.' Religious men would, of course, wear their *kappels* (prayer caps) in bed unlike the women, who removed their *sheitels* (wigs).

Younger children sometimes slept in their parents' room in a pull-out bed known as the *schlufbank*. Babies always slept with their parents. If cribs or cots were unaffordable, upturned drawers or orange boxes served the same purpose. In fact, orange boxes were used to store clothes, too. People had few clothes. 'Best' outfits were hung on hooks or on backs of doors in readiness for *Shabbat* and in most cases one set of school garments sufficed. Notwithstanding the fact that adults seldom slept alone, children never saw their parents naked and seldom cuddled up to them in bed. Propriety was always observed.

Siblings usually shared beds: there might be two or three at the top and two or three at the bottom – an arrangement affectionately known as sleeping *kopf zu fuss*. Each family member had his/her fixed position in the bed and there was usually a pecking order that worked according to age and bedtime. Sid was the eldest in his family and his sisters and brothers guarded his position –

'Sid's position' – in the bed for him every time he went out dancing and returned home late. In desperate times, lodgers, who might sleep in the same room as the younger members of the family, were accommodated for reduced rates. As far as possible, boys and girls slept in separate rooms. If a child was a bed wetter or unwell his/her siblings accommodated him/her just the same. A lady told us that she always slept at the bottom of her parents' bed. This arrangement lasted until the older of her two sisters left home to be married, when, at last, she was able to leave her parents' bed and move in with her remaining sister. Another family slept seven in a room: parents in one bed and five brothers and sisters in another. If you slept in the middle of a bed and had to wake, you nudged your fellow sleepers, who 'rolled over' to accommodate your needs. There was no oversleeping. Spartan, unheated bedrooms could be cold and unfriendly in winter and often smelled of iodine, which was used as a cure against chilblains. In summer, these rooms were hot and sometimes infested with bedbugs. Reading in bed, 'lying in' and, most of all, privacy, were unheard-of luxuries.

Beds were usually covered with feathered covers that resembled duvets and were called *paranas* or *uberdecks*. These were stuffed with eiderdown or goose feathers – called *pooch* – and were often family heirlooms brought out of the *heim*. All the feathers seemed to travel to one end of the *paranas*, but, despite this, these covers were warm and comforting! Sheets and blankets, which came later, were considered modern and were favoured by newlyweds, who might buy them from Wickhams and Blundells or 'the very good bedding shop' in Hessel Street. No sheets were used beneath *paranas*. Blankets – when used – were usually cream or grey. During the War and while rationing applied, cream blankets with special utility marks on them were issued to young married couples. Those who lacked money enough for blankets piled coats on top of themselves for warmth. Blankets were stored in trunks or blanket boxes in the summer. Those lucky enough to possess wardrobes stored blankets in large bottom drawers. These were often lined with newspapers.

Mattresses were thick and often lumpy and made of horsehair or flock with open springs. They were usually covered with ticking.

Linen or cotton sheets were used in summer and flannel in the winter. Whatever fabric was used in chilly bedrooms, bed linen always felt cold. Pillows were usually a metre square and shared among the bed's many occupants. A lady told us of her devoted, but impoverished, mother who cut her own pillow in two so that her daughter might have two pillows, stuffed with feathers from the *heim* as part of her dowry. In addition to pillows, people sometimes used bolsters, which propped sleepers up in an almost upright position and were not always very comfortable.

Sheets were usually washed either weekly or fortnightly and were sent to local laundries such as Sussex Laundry for this purpose. Some families sent their sheets to washerwomen who washed and ironed or, simply, washed and returned sheets wet, for home drying, where they were always folded before being mangled to save effort on the ironing. All this was time-consuming and exhausting. Some people economised by 'topping and tailing' – which meant turning sheets around and washing them every other week.

After a night's sleep, families climbed out of warm beds onto cold floors that were usually covered with boards. These were stained or, in the more well-to-do households, adorned with carpet squares. Lino was the most popular floor covering, despite being cold and slippery. It was usually beige or brown and was laid over newspaper, which was used as underlay. By the late 1940s, fitted carpet was used in bedrooms.

When war broke out, families left the pleasures and privations of shared sleeping to fight for and support their country. Cosy domesticity and household routine were never the same again.

Life Behind Closed Doors

Life behind closed doors was not always as it seemed and house-holders' resourcefulness knew no bounds.

Can *you* think of 25 uses for newspaper?

- Toilet paper: although newspaper sometimes blocked the toilet, the print never came off!
- To wrap waste and rubbish before discarding it in the bin.
- To line drawers and shelves.
- To cover the white tablecloth used on the *Shabbat* so that it would be clean when required.
- To line cupboards: the newspaper was changed once a year – usually before *Pesach*.
- To stuff into gaps in floorboards in order to keep out draughts and dust.
- To line floors before lino or carpet were laid.
- To catch drips from wet washing.
- To cover 'just washed' floors.
- To envelop the heated lid of a saucepan which was used to warm beds.
- To clean windows with vinegar and water, which guaranteed no smears.
- To cover sweaters prior to ironing.
- To stuff into toes of shoes which were too large.
- To be folded into a cone shape and used in sweet shops and grocery stores as receptacles for sweets, rice, sugar, broken biscuits and other dry goods.

- To wrap fish and chips.
- To wrap herrings for cooking on makeshift fires for workroom lunches.
- To wrap vegetables and line shopping bags at a market stall.
- To scrunch up into balls and place on grates with wood or coal for kindling.
- To cover windows of rooms being decorated so that no one could see inside.
- To fold into hat shapes and use to protect bald heads, particularly, against the sun.
- To roll up and use as a fly swatter.
- To cover books and preserve their covers.
- To make sailing boats for children to sail in baths or gutters.
- To protect the shoulders of customers being shaved in barbershops.

Even to READ! The *Daily Herald* and *News Chronicle* were the popular papers; *The Star* gave racing results for horses and the dogs; Yiddish newspapers carried advertisements which promised employment to prospective sons-in-law; the *Daily Worker* was the communist newspaper; the *Daily Mail* backed Oswald Mosley at the start of his campaign; *The Graphic* and *The Sketch* were the liberal papers; *The Standard* was one of the London evening papers and *The News of the World* was risqué and told of sex scandals.

In the East End Jewish community, domestic life ran like a well-oiled machine and, as the imaginative use of newspaper suggests, householders were resourceful and managed their houses with skill and dedication. Mother was usually in charge and did most of the heavy work in the house. She made the beds and prepared the breakfast, she cooked lunches for her children and bathed them in tin baths that she carried, emptied and filled. If she could not afford to send her laundry to Sussex Laundry, she boiled water on the cooker for washing and fed sheets through the mangle on washday Mondays. On wintry days, she hung washing from a line suspended from the ceiling so that it could dry before the fire. Although her daughters sometimes helped her with household chores, mother did all the cooking herself. On some Thursday nights she made *lockshen* and hung it over chairs to dry. She cooked the chicken soup, baked, prepared for the *Shabbat* and sent her children to play in the streets to afford her space and privacy.

The focus of many a housewife's industry was the black range in the kitchen. These ranges were installed at no cost by the LCC and kept houses warm in winter. Summer months told a different story and the oppressive heat in kitchens led to infestations of *vanzen* that drove people out of doors. Some lucky housewives had a kitchen and a scullery, which was a small side area for dirty work which often smelled of carbolic and damp from wet washing, and which housed the 'copper' (the boiler), the gas cooker – if there was one – and a brown stone sink with cold running water. Father sometimes shaved in this sink and the *shmutters* (cleaning cloths) were washed in it. If nowhere else was available, the entire family congregated in the scullery to wash. Some sculleries contained cupboards for storage, but in kosher households, where two sets of everything were required (one for meat and one for milk) orange boxes – which also sometimes doubled as furniture – were often used for storage. Some families had dressers where they proudly displayed their willow pattern china, perhaps, or their tin mugs for 'every day.' Milkmen sometimes gave away china plates, cups and saucers every time housewives introduced them to new customers. A man told us that his father moved the dresser aside so that he could paint the wall behind it. The dresser was not properly replaced and it fell over, smashing all the china on it. Only the *Pesach* china stored in the orange boxes remained. This was a tragedy!

Mother was dependent on the money father gave her and most families were too poor for mother even to think of buying anything for – or sometimes even feeding – herself. Some women and children worked at home for a pittance by sewing buttonholes or making clothes for private customers. Most families had at least one member who gambled and wives of gamblers often received little or no money at all. A lady told us she was sure her father would gladly have sold her to pay for a bet. She and her brother eventually persuaded their mother to evict him – which was rare in Jewish families. Families often put money aside for 'a rainy day' or the tallyman and they sometimes kept this money in tin boxes or jars called *knippels*, which they kept well hidden. A lady told us that she was so angered by the fact that her husband spent his entire wages on gambling that she approached his boss to suggest he pay her directly. He refused, so she stood outside the factory gates and fought with her husband, who relented slightly and gave her some money. Alas, she knew that her husband would go off to the dogs and spend the rest of his pay packet on betting.

BETTING SLIPS UNDER MATTRESS.

◆

POLICE RAID A BOW HOUSE.

As the result of a police raid, Maud Beatrice Hunt, 50, a widow, and George Hunt, 29, a labourer, both of 36 Ranwell-street, Bow, were charged at Old-street Police Court yesterday with being found on premises at that address alleged to be used as a betting house. George Hunt was also charged with using the premises for the purpose of betting, and Maud Hunt with permitting them to be so used.

Inspector George Pett, of H Division, said he entered the premises on Monday, saw prisoners, and read a warrant to them. The male prisoner said "Not me; he has gone." Witness told them he would search the house from top to bottom, and the male prisoner said "All right, I will show you where they are," and entered a bedroom on the ground floor. He lifted up a mattress, and in an envelope witness found seventeen betting slips When told she would be arrested for permitting the premises to be used for the purpose of betting Mrs. Hunt said "What for? I was in the kitchen."

In cross-examination by Mr. A. E. Robinson (who defended and who had stated that he was prepared to plead guilty to street betting in the case of George Hunt), the officer said Mrs. Hunt was a respectable woman who had been living in the house a number of years.

P.S. Stephens, 45 H, gave evidence as to keeping observation on the premises on three dates and seeing George Hunt, who was standing inside a passage, take slips and what appeared to be money from men, women and children.

The magistrate (Mr. Langley) discharged Mrs. Hunt and, convicting George Hunt of street betting, ordered him to pay a fine of £5 and £5 10s, costs.

23. Gambling posed a real problem for families who were already struggling to exist on meagre incomes, 1936. [Courtesy of the British Museum Newspaper Library, Colindale.]

A few women joined their husbands at the dogs, but most spent the little leisure time they had gossiping with neighbours, darning, crocheting or, on rare occasions, playing cards at home. Friday nights were often card nights – for men, particularly – and favourite games were Kanasta, Pontoon, Pisha Paisha and Klubyosh. Card games, not to mention Baccarat and Roulette, were often played for high stakes and cabinetmakers and tailors were reputed to be especially big gamblers. A lady told us that her father went off gambling the night before her brother's bar mitzvah despite her mother's entreaties. The daughter was sent to retrieve him and threatened to scream at him outside the gambling den until the neighbours knew about it. The guilty father soon emerged. Men who knew little English seemed to know enough to place a bet. They often used young boys who stood on street corners as runners between them and the often illegal bookmakers who traded as far away as possible from policemen's prying eyes.

Some couples went to the Yiddish Theatre and some independent women went to the pictures alone or with one of the children who could read the subtitles out loud. A man remembered hearing his mother explain in broken English to his father the story of a film she had seen in his absence. Most of the time, however, women were housebound and their men and boys were little help. There was a pecking order in many households where the oldest daughters bore the most stressful domestic burdens and the youngest the least. Some men chopped up orange boxes for firewood or brought in coal for fires. Most fathers worked such long hours that they were rarely at home – let alone there to offer help – except in the slack season when they gave their wives cause to grumble by being home too much! Out-of-work tailors hung around the Gas Show Rooms outside the Tailors' Union, playing cards and hoping to be extracted by employers seeking casual labour. A man told us that he helped his wife with the cleaning at the start of his marriage. His mother visited and told his wife in no uncertain terms that she had not brought her son up to do housework. The son crept out of the house, leaving the women to resolve the matter. If a man were caught helping his wife with domestic chores what would the neighbours think?

The majority of parents never talked intimately in front of their children and cuddles and hugs were a rarity. Most households were run by rules which mother made and father enforced. It was not uncommon for bullying to take place in families. Father bullied mother and children, who were afraid to disobey him, and older siblings sometimes bullied the younger ones. The threat of the belt was used but rarely put into practice. A man told us that his father gave him 1s 6d to pay for *cheder*. The son stopped at a pontoon game *en route* and lost his father's money. When he returned home, his father asked to see the receipt from Mr Lipchitz the *cheder* teacher who had contacted him enquiring after his son's whereabouts. When the lying boy told his father he had left the receipt in the classroom, the threat of the belt became a reality! A lady told us how her mother and father seldom walked out together. On the occasions that they did, the father always walked in front of his wife. The couple rarely communicated and showed little love for each other. However, to the extent that they had eight children together, 'something must have happened!' Children often knew nothing of their mothers' pregnancies until the baby arrived. No child ever asked where babies came from: this was a life behind closed doors.

The shame of divorce or separation and the fear of neighbour's opinions kept many an unhappy marriage from falling apart. Parents often spoke Yiddish, Russian or Romanian in front of their children to protect them from anguish, and *'nicht in front of die kinder'* was a common expression. Whatever the turmoil at home, there were always two family faces: one 'for the neighbours' and one for 'indoors'. A man told us that his family fried bacon for breakfast every Sunday morning. One day the Orthodox grandfather knocked on the door to say he could smell what they were cooking. No one dared open the door. What if the neighbours heard their row? Another family kept arguing over finances. The father had a grocery store but he treated his customers badly. His wife exacerbated the situation by shouting at him in front of the customers for treating them 'like dirt'! A man told us that his aunt was always spoken of in hushed tones behind closed doors. She had 'misbehaved' with a gentleman. The family hounded the poor woman until she left for Australia: she had shamed them 'in front of the neighbours.'

'Ought To Be Dipped In Duck Pond'

MAGISTRATE REBUKES CLAPTON FAMILIES

After hearing a number of witnesse.
In a case in which Mrs. Rose Cohen, o
28 Forburg-road, Clapton, summoned
Mrs. Lillian Collins, of the same address
for assault, the North London magis
trate (Mr. W. Blake Odgers, K.C.) or
Tuesday told them they all ought to be
" dipped in the duck pond."

"This case is an even more disgracefu
exhibition than the ones I usually get
in this Court," he declared. " Here are
two families, both of the Jewish faith
living in the same house, who don't
make the slightest attempt to live together in peace. They all talk far too
much, and shout and scream, instead
of talking in a normal voice. As soor.
as this sort of thing begins, someone
starts resorting to violence. The women
tear each other's hair out, and the men
start fighting. It's perfectly disgraceful
The whole lot of you ought to be dipped
in the duck pond for behaving like a
lot of ill-tempered, spiteful, bad-
mannered children."

24. Efforts at maintaining a 'public face' were not always successful. *Hackney Gazette*, 1938.

Parents never 'talked money' in their children's presence and extreme poverty was a source of shame. Visits to soup kitchens were hidden 'from the neighbours' and children, who prayed that their friends might not see them, were often sent out to fetch the soup and bread provided. There was no state money to claim and offers of help from the Board of Guardians were humiliating. The really desperate went to pawnbrokers as a last resort but never spoke of these visits.

Whatever the circumstances, and as long as families kept their dignity, life continued. You worked resiliently to make the best of your lot and exploited your chances. However difficult home life was, there was always life on the streets...

25. The soup kitchen for the Jewish poor in Brune Street – now a luxury block of flats.

Life on the Streets

To an outsider looking in, it seemed that life on the streets was lived in technicolor – like a painting come to life. Jewish immigrants arrived at the London Docks from all over Europe and were drawn to places where their fellow Jews lived and where they could congregate together to form communities, which replicated – as far as possible – their former way of life. Because housing conditions in the East End were often severely cramped and inhospitable and because there were no distractions like television sets, computers or stereos to lure people indoors, families established an elaborate system of outdoor networks. Pre-war streets belonged to the people. Deals were done, games played, friendships made, and hierarchies established, on residential streets which were virtually undisturbed by traffic.

East End community spirit was strong. If there was a bereavement in a family – be it Jewish or not – people living on the same street would care for the children and bring food to the mourning relatives. When a baby was born everyone on the street rallied round to look after the older siblings. On public celebrations, such as Empire Day, children came home early from school and joined their parents in street celebrations. Street life followed patterns; its changing landscape was coloured by events, seasons, days of the week and times of day.

During the week, the streets were peopled with traders and the housewife's routine was shaped by calls from servicemen, sales-

67

"A DELIBERATE FRAUD ON THE POOR."

Milk Dealer Fined £50.

Fines of £50 and 40s., respectively together with costs amounting to six guineas, were imposed at Old-street Police Court on Tuesday on Bert Davies, of 231, Kingsland-road, who was summoned for selling milk that contained 76 per cent. less than the proper amount of fat, and also for selling milk from a vehicle and receptacle neither of which was inscribed with his name and address.

Two assistants to the inspector gave evidence as to defendant supplying a pint of milk for 3d. and calling out, "Pure dairy farm milk; very good milk."

Defendant, on oath, produced a label that he contended was on the churn, and which could be seen by all the public.

Mr. Clarke Hall said it was a very bad case indeed—a deliberate fraud on poor people, who found it difficult to buy milk at present prices.

Mr Margetts, prosecuting for the Bethnal Green Borough Council, mentioned that there was a previous conviction.

26. *Hackney Gazette*, March 1922.

men and hawkers selling wares. Her day might begin as early as 5 a.m. with the purchase of fresh bread or an onion *platzel* from a local street baker or bagels from Esther, the bagel queen, who sat at Bloom's Corner, Brick Lane. Esther was a well-known character who hurled abuse at her arch-rival, Annie, who also sold bagels a few yards away. Busy householders were well supported by traders who traded door-to-door, as well as by those who stood on street corners. There was always a feeling of the street in the house and the house in the street. Milkmen would go into larders to see what was needed. Housewives lined up outside to fill their jugs from the milkmen's churns. Postmen announced their approach with a thud of black boots on cobblestones. They made four or five daily deliveries and, on lazy days, stayed for tea. Really important news – whether good or bad – was delivered by telegram boys on bicycles. Dustmen, who always seemed to wear their caps backwards, walked casually through houses from the front door to the back yard to collect the rubbish. Those in the community who lived in high flats – and could not avail themselves of this service – occasionally threw garbage directly onto the streets. 'If you were unlucky you might have a load of *kishkes* (chicken's entrails) wrapped in newspaper land directly on your head!' In the summer months the iceman delivered ice, which he carried on his back and cut up with a hammer, to housewives who would otherwise have found preserving food impossible. Laundrymen made weekly collections of laundry, the coalman delivered coal and the chipman visited twice-weekly to sell bundles of wood wrapped in wire. The catmeat man threw the cat food into the cellar or dropped it through the letterbox. The tallyman collected housewives' savings put aside for household luxuries. He would leave bundles of towels, sheets or other luxuries on doorsteps by way of temptation, and found that housewives usually succumbed! A lady told us that she and her friends paid the tallyman 'on the never-never'. Why 'the never-never'? 'Because one purchase led to another and you never finished paying: the forerunner to the credit card!'

There were persistent insurance salesmen and door-to-door dress salesmen, who used the gift of the gab to seduce householders into paying exorbitant prices for inferior merchandise. The empty bottle collector did as his name suggested and rewarded children with a ride on his cart if they gave him empty lemonade bottles. The tin man collected tin and the rag and bone man gave out goldfish or odd plates in place of cash for scrap metal – 'any old iron.' The muffin man carried his tray of muffins on his head and announced his presence with a bell. Bob Strong was a well-known street character who had a stall in Petticoat Lane market and also paid door-to-door visits selling pills: 'Dutch drops for half a crown.' His patter went: 'A spoonful of phospherine will cure you – corns, coughs, bones in the leg!' Somehow, his elixir always worked!

At lunchtime and, again, after four o'clock, the streets filled with chattering children returning home from school or running outside to play. As parents worked hard and lacked time to talk, their children had to become self-reliant, resourceful and streetwise. Aside from conventional favourites, like hopscotch, cricket and rounders, necessity often forced children to play games of their own invention with tins, pieces of wood, or pieces of string. They gave these games names like 'Tiles,' 'Tibby,' 'Cannon' or 'Diablo.' 'Knocking Down Ginger' was a popular game. Children knocked on doors and ran away leaving irate parents peering from doorways into empty streets. Girls with swinging plaits and pinafores tucked into knickers sometimes made their own dolls out of sticks and cloths with mop heads for faces. Boys in shorts played *glarneys* (marbles) in gutters or converted apple boxes into carts or dolls' prams by fitting them with wheels. Trading instincts started young and the owners of these carts sometimes charged other children to ride on them. 'Look behind you, governor' was a game played by boys who hung onto the back of horse-driven carts until the driver screamed 'ger'off'! Parents sometimes used their children as part of street management. Young boys occasionally acted as 'lookout' for illegal bookmakers in Brick Lane and some children were sent out to check that street traders were working properly. A man remembered being sent out to pick up stray lumps of coal that had dropped out of coalmen's sacks after deliveries and several people remembered being instructed, as children, to check that chimney sweeps were doing their job properly and that their brooms were sticking out of the tops of chimney pots before parents 'paid up.' The Jewish community was not a drinking one. People remembered seeing non-Jewish children patiently sitting on the kerb outside pubs – which were often no more than rooms in houses where jugs of beer were sold – waiting for their parents to emerge. A horse and cart would spray the streets 'to clean the air' from time to time – with little effect. Young boys jumped in and out of the water or hitched a ride on the cart.

Girls usually helped their mothers prepare for *Shabbat* with cooking, cleaning, darning and ironing or polishing the black lead grate and whitening the front step. When their mothers had moments of free time, they might sit on their doorsteps to gossip. Doors were left open and keys swung from string tied to door-knockers. This was a trusting community and, somehow, people always felt safe. Even if you missed the last bus and had a long walk home, the worst you might chance upon were drunken men lying in gutters after pub closing hours. Policemen, who were respected and trusted, but not, it has to be said, above accepting the occasional bribe, patrolled the streets – usually in pairs. If a boy kicked a ball into an unfortunate's window, the policeman on the beat would blow his whistle and caution him. Moishe Glazier, a well-known street trader who carried window frames on his back, would be summoned to repair the damage at a cost of three-pence or sixpence for every broken windowpane! A lady told us that policemen accepted bananas from her father's grocer shop in return for allowing him to trade after hours. The only police-man out of the 80 or so working at the docks who would *not* accept bribes was called a 'rotter'! Several Jewish traders were affection-ately known as 'Moishe' (Moses) – a tradition that may have orig-inated in the *heim*. Moishe Glazier worked alongside Moishe Chicken, who sold live kosher chickens in the street as well as the market for 11d a pound. His lady assistant removed the feathers and cleaned the chickens so that housewives could inspect them for plumpness. Moishe Taster sold toffee on a barrow outside school gates. He called his mixed bag of toffee 'The Jubilee Mix.' Children would chant 'Moishe, Moishe give me a taster,' and he would break off pieces of toffee for them with his *Hackmesser* (hammer) while *daverning*! Some of the community's more enter-prising members played two, or more, roles in the street: Benjy Cokeman delivered both coke and coal, and moved people's furniture with a horse and cart; Mr Stern, fruit seller in Brick Lane, doubled as 'official' matchmaker; and Harry Brooks, respected Mayor of Bethnal Green, supplemented his income by sweeping chimneys from time to time.

At weekends, great crowds of youngsters strolled through the streets in search of 'talent' – a ritual known as the 'Monkey Parade.'

Triple Dangers in the East End.

◆

To the Editor of THE JEWISH CHRONICLE.

Sir,—Being brought daily into close contact with life in East London in all its stark reality, I realise only too clearly that I am witnessing nemesis slowly overtaking London Jewry, and, to my horror, seeing the disintegration of Jewish family life.

Let us not close our eyes any more to facts. The average young Jewish boy or girl after leaving school and coming out into the world, is drifting away more perceptibly than ever from Jewish influence. Yet practically nothing is being done for them. Unless they form clubs and societies of their own volition, hardly any outside guidance is being brought to bear to assist them religiously, morally, educationally or culturally. Any efforts which are at all being made are small and meagre in scope and paltry in effect, with the one exception, that of Mr. Basil Henriques. No one appreciates more than the writer the excellent *social* work which Mr. Henriques and his devoted wife are doing in East London. I am, however, more than ever convinced that Mr. Henriques's religious work is resulting in the weakening of the Jewish bond, and consequent cleavage in Jewish families. The very teachings he enunciates set up differences between parents and children, as what he advocates is the very negation of the ideals so many of us cherish and hold dear.

The second danger is the street-corner lounging, and the "Whitechapel Parade," with its unwholesome mixing of the sexes by means of casual street acquaintances, a state of affairs far more prevalent in this locality that in any other part of the metropolis. The result is that it is the high road to moral turpitude and laxity.

The "Liberal" movement is leading to the apostate's gate ; the "Whitechapel Parade" to indifference. Which is the worse I dare not imagine.

The one who is to blame is the smugly complacent, so-called orthodox Jew, who does nothing for social welfare, not even guiding his own children. He will probably shrug his shoulders when he sees his neighbours' children straying. What is this orthodox Jew doing for the well-being of Young Jewry which he is supposed to have at heart ? He is immune from criticism, beyond perhaps lifting his hands heavenwards in pious exhortation, with, maybe, an imprecation on his lips for the malignant forces which he does nothing to contend with. Why does orthodox Jewry stay in the background and refuse to lift a finger to succour or aid where it is so sorely needed ? This, too, is one of our great dangers.—I am, &c.,

A SOCIAL WORKER.

27. The 'Monkey Parade' aroused much moral concern among the more traditional members of the Jewish community. *The Jewish Chronicle*, 15 March 1929.

72

On Saturday nights the streets were peopled with families return-ing from football matches or visits to the West End or teenagers coming home after a dance. During the 1930s the recession drove people, who might have been otherwise employed, onto the streets to 'earn a bob or two.' Desperation often turned out-of-work traders and professionals into street entertainers. Characters like Solomon Levy, for example, sang 'I'm a true-born Yiddish man' to whomsoever cared to listen. Some East End street entertainers like Wilson, Kappel and Betty, found fame in the wider world. This trio invented the 'Sand Dance' and were affectionately known as 'Cleopatra's nightmare.'

Joe Coral, in London, aged 92. Bookmaker and founder of a bet-ting shop and leisure group chain, he was born Joseph Kagarlitski in Poland and brought as a child to London by his widowed mother before the First World War. As a 14-year-old school leaver, moon-lighting as a bookie's runner, he realised the potential and used his barmitzvah money to set him-self up. The business flourished when off-course cash betting be-came legal in the 1960s.

28. The obituary of Joe Coral. Joe Coral worked his way up from runner for illegal bookies to owner of the largest chain of betting shops in the UK. [Courtesy of *The Jewish Chronicle*.]

Larger-than-life eccentrics defied poverty and wove their way into the tapestry of street life merely by standing out from the norm. Some of those remembered with affection were Prince Monolulu, a self-proclaimed Abyssinian prince and racing tipster who lived in Whitechapel and paraded the streets dressed in 'real suede and real leather' crying, 'I've got a horse! I've got a horse!;' Aran, the one-time tailor with hair down his back who made a daily, silent, pilgrimage from Hyde Park to Commercial Road and back; and Katy 'Warhorse,' who did occasional scrubbing and cleaning in the community, 'had the largest hooter you ever saw' and 'was definitely more like a man!' Characters such as Mike Stern auctioned crockery and attracted large crowds with his plate throwing and his patter; Ted Kid Berg, the famous Jewish boxer, practised on the streets; and Tubby and Barney Isaacs entered street folklore as purveyors of jellied eels.

When war broke out, this mutually supportive community was turned on its head and patterns of life were shattered. The Jewish

73

immigrants joined their compatriots in battle and were forced to abandon a way of life that had retained so many elements from the *heim*. In the fullness of time, everything changed – as all things must. Supermarkets replaced street vendors, and telephones street gossip. Doors – once open – were now firmly locked. People moved away from the East End of London to houses with gardens and children played in privacy. The disappearance of life on the streets broke many threads of continuity and support from the Jewish community's heritage. We lament this.

29. Derby Day, 1936. Gypsies, tipsters (including Prince Monolulu to the left), hawkers and entertainers at Epsom for the famous race. [Courtesy of the British Museum Newspaper Library, Colindale.]

Markets

In the world before the War, the 'market' might be a small shop, a stall, a wheelbarrow, a makeshift stand outside a shop, or even a tray hanging from a seller's neck. If a widow was left penniless, she might establish a 'market' by opening her front room window and selling her possessions to passers-by. Markets were central to most peoples' lives – as far as both shopping and entertainment were concerned – and this applied especially in the East End where there seemed to be a market on nearly every residential street and commercial area.

Markets were usually lively, bustling places, many of which stayed open late when, in winter months, they took on a warm eerie glow from paraffin and gas lamps. Some markets remained open for business all the year round, including Christmas Day. Markets provided a feast for the senses: the smell of live chickens mingled with fruiterer's cries like – *'Weibe, weibe, die beste is here'* – and there were escapologists, barrel organ players with monkeys on their shoulders and jugglers selling china plates that never seemed to break. The distinction between trade and entertainment was finely drawn. Some market traders sold funeral coats to non-Jewish people, and others dressed up in women's clothes 'just to show how good they looked.' There was the market 'trader' who did nothing more than 'guess your weight': you paid him only if, after prodding and peering, he scored a bull's eye! Marie Cohen sold clothes from a stall in Watney Street. The clothes were piled on a sheet on the floor and you could not try them on. Her

30. Second-hand clothes could be bought at Cheepen, 32 Bath Street, Clerkenwell, EC1.

patter went, 'Show the lady that model – here's the front, here's the back.' One man remembered seeing a lady disappear in a dress she had tried on behind a van next to his stall. The fact that she had left him her old dress was no consolation at all. There was the trader who sold only birds – such as parrots – and rabbits; Dan Pickle sold pickles; and the Cat Meat Man in Brick Lane sold cat meat – as one might expect. A fruit man in Portabello Road market used to boil his oranges to make them look bigger – 'when you brought them home and peeled them, they were half empty inside!' Mrs Marks sold herrings in Petticoat Lane. Her speciality was barrels of *schmaltz* herring that she sold for three pennies a herring and handed to her customers wrapped up in newspaper. A lady remembered her uncle's curtain remnants and linen stall. The uncle acted like an auctioneer, selling handkerchiefs in packets of four for a shilling, or 'extra special' ones, which were no different from the others, in packets of three for the same price. One Jack Cohen started life with a tray of anything around his neck and a stall in Islington that he stocked with unlabelled tins, or 'seconds.' These tins sometimes caused confusion – 'you bought what you thought was a tin of cocoa in the market and found that it was a tin of cat food by the time you arrived back home!' The same Jack Cohen later founded Tesco – an acronym formed from Tessa and Cohen – the first supermarket to be opened in the United Kingdom.

East End market traders, who worked hard, showed initiative and were nearly always wealthy, were considered eligible as prospective husbands. Unfortunately, they occasionally exploited housewives' gullible natures to make easy money – 'a *metzee-er* for a bargain' – as their patter often went. Transactions were usually done in cash, tax was seldom paid – 'a taxman's nightmare' – and 'fiddling' was quite common. In Middlesex Street, one Jackie Brauffman went to clothing manufacturers to buy 'cabbage' (leftover garments) in bulk. He auctioned these at his market stall for about 'one guinea a dress' and attracted large crowds with his irresistible patter. Jackie's 'eye for the best numbers' meant that he became one of the market boys who 'made big money'. He drove around everywhere in his shiny Rolls Royce as testimony to his achievements. Notwithstanding all this, a lady from North London told us that her brother would not allow her to marry her fiancé, a successful East End market trader called Bob Strong, strong man and purveyor of medicines, because he considered him unworthy of their family.

Stallholders needed to obtain licences from the local council in order to operate, but some of the more unscrupulous did not bother. 'There were ways round this,' they said. Some traders sold fruit, for example, at night time, when 'there were no coppers about' and some sold goods – such as mismatched stockings – from suitcases which mysteriously disappeared (together with their owners) when customers returned with their complaints. Although policemen occasionally 'made examples' and sent wrongdoers to prison, they usually 'turned a blind eye' to illegal trading: they had enough to do. Occasionally, *schleppers* were employed to stand on pavements outside shops or lean against stalls to encourage potential shoppers. These men could be quite intimidating and difficult to avoid. They had a patter all of their own which often went something like 'have we got something special just for you!' One of the market traders' superstitions was that you should never let the first customer go. Any shopper wanting a good bargain knew that it was necessary to arrive early and bargain hard for a low price. There seemed to be two rules of thumb for customers: you had to bargain and you had to queue. Long queues often formed at market stalls and people sometimes joined them first, then asked, 'why are we queuing?' As far as bargaining was concerned, every stallholder added a little to his prices to allow for 'special' reductions. On the whole, haggling over prices was quite good-natured and customers would know

BLACK MARKET DELINGS

---❖---

Illegal Transactions In Poultry and Eggs

At Bow-street Magistrates' Court on Tuesday a poultry dealer, Richard Reeder, of High-road, Pitsea, Essex, was fined £200, with £15 15s. costs for selling 31 chickens, without a licence and delivering them without a prescribed declaration.

Henry Potter, a dealer, of 9 Glenarm-road, Clapton, was fined £45, and ordered to pay £5 5s. costs for taking delivery of the chickens without a declaration and selling them at an excessive price.

Potter was also fined £250, with £15 15s. costs, for buying 2,340 eggs from an unknown man without a licence.

Leonard Delamere, butcher, of 253 Well-street, Hackney, who obtained the chickens from Potter for £21, was fined £15 for buying them at an excessive price and otherwise than by weight. He was also ordered to pay £5 5s. costs.

The magistrate (Mr. Sidney Marks) said he had no doubt Potter was a member of a ring who had been dealing hard in the black market.

31. The 'Black Market' flourished during the War. *Hackney Gazette*, 16 January 1948.

that lowest possible prices had been reached when stallholders refused to sell. Traders usually wrapped sold goods in brown paper, newspaper or paper bags; and string bags (bought in the market), which frequently broke – leaving purchases scattered all over the streets – were the favoured way of transporting shopping.

During the War, another kind of market flourished and that was the 'black market.' For money, you could find anything – and the grapevine of gossip led you to so-and-so for clothes or a friend of a friend for, say, eggs. People suffered more in London and other big towns than in the country and on farms, and there was a countrywide shortage of luxury items such as silk stockings, chocolates, sweets, beef cubes and tins of fruit. Occasionally, women whose husbands were away 'at the front' managed to persuade stallholders to give them 'something special' – like meat or eggs which had been kept 'under the counter' – when their husbands came home on leave. These 'special' eggs were nowhere to be found when policemen were about.

Some markets were wholly Jewish, some mixed – with Jewish and non-Jewish traders in them – and some had no Jewish connection at all. Jewish markets such as Hessel Street and Brick Lane Markets had to close on Saturdays and – unlike their non-Jewish counter-parts, where you could buy jellied eels, mussels and whelks – usually sold kosher chickens and herrings. It was said that no Jewish woman worth her salt would buy a chicken 'before she had stuck her hand up its backside to see if it had plenty of *schmaltz* and all the giblets and liver intact.' Other of the many markets included the animal market at Club Row which sold speciality animals – 'if you fancied a talking parrot you went there;' Ridley Road market, where you could buy 'good poultry;' Leather Lane market in the City which sold everything from toys to suitcases; Jubilee Street market; Jamaica Street market; Petticoat Lane market, which was a popular Sunday destination and where characters like Bob Strong and his sons, or Mrs Marks and Tubby Isaacs – both of them fishmongers – operated; Hare Street and Cobb Street markets; Berwick Street market in the West End, where there were shops and stalls outside them selling mainly clothes; Chapel Street in Islington, where Jack Cohen started trading; and Watney Street

32. Abraham Smith's butcher shop, 68 Brushfield Street. (His previous premises in Princes Street, Spitalfields, had burnt down.)

33. D. Ackerman & Sons jewellery shop, 11 Greenfield Street.

34. M. Boxer Wholesale Provision Merchant.

market off Commercial Road, which was good for shoes. Cabi-netmakers traditionally bought their aprons for sixpence each at Brick Lane Market; and a lady remembered her grandmother buy-ing 'wet fish' – that is to say, live fish – from a tank in Petticoat Lane and taking it home in a large bottle filled with water. Every-thing you could imagine was sold in markets – from meat to cur-tains, animals to handkerchiefs and stockings to live fish! Unfor-tunately, some customers were so poverty stricken, that they even took home with them for extra bedding the discarded straw that had protected china packed in crates.

Markets formed part of the lifeblood of the community. You might not be able to have goods delivered or to 'pay on tick' – as you might do if you bought from a shop – but there were bargains to be found and your spirits were often lifted with a laugh. If nothing else, markets connected you to your community – and that was always a good thing.

Away from it All

Leisure activities provided another life away from overcrowded homes with few comforts. The main exit routes were dancing, youth clubs, visits to the 'pictures,' the Yiddish Theatre and outings to parks and the seaside. For the majority of youngsters the best leisure activity was dancing. Dancing afforded fantasy, excitement, music, and, of course, an opportunity for close contact with members of the opposite sex. Some young men and women went dancing as often as two or three times a week and usually paid 2s 6d on Saturday nights or 1s 6d on other nights for the privilege.

Most teenagers began to go dancing at the ages of 14 or 15, when some had just joined the workforce and their mothers permitted them to keep enough money back from their wages to afford visits to the dancehalls. Among the favourite venues were The Lyceum – a one-time theatre – with its sloping dance floor: 'while dancing down was not bad, dancing uphill was quite hard work!'; and the Streatham Locarno, which accommodated up to 4,000 dancers at a time and ran a coach from the East End to the hall for one shilling, and where Dog Swallow and his orchestra played. Dances were demonstrated and taught at the Royal at Tottenham, and the Trocadero was the place to go for tea and dinner dances. Lou Prager played at Hammersmith Palais, Snakehip Johnson and Al Boley at the Café Royal, and the famed Joe Loss at the Astoria, Tottenham Court Road.

☞ JOE LOSS AND HIS BAND
IN ATTENDANCE *Somewhere 9. England* ☜

MODERNITES
Social and Sports Club.

Present

✍ DANCING TIME FOR DANCERS ✍

EVERY THURSDAY
From 7 - 11 pm.

at the

KING'S HALL 83-85 Commercial Rd. E.1
IMAIN HALLI.

THIS WEEK – MORE FREE PRIZES
𝔇ancing to 𝔄 𝔉irst 𝔠lass 𝔅and
ADMISSION NINEPENCE

TICKETS OBTAINABLE from The Adonion Press, 26, Elder Street, Commercial St. E.1 .

35. Joe Loss was one of the most popular band leaders of the 1940s. [Courtesy of the British Museum Newspaper Library, Colindale.]

Although there was always the one who refused to go 'dancing and prancing' and was 'content to meet a future spouse through a matchmaker,' most youngsters embraced dancing with meticulous attention to detail in the preparation and great delight in the execution. Girls, smelling of 'Soir de Paris' perfume, would wear their finest frocks and put on their make-up with care. Those who applied their make-up in cloakrooms away from parents' prying eyes, stood in rows in front of mirrors, moistening solid blocks of mascara with spit or painting black beauty spots onto their faces so as to 'look like the film star, Claudette Colbert.' Stilettos were not allowed on dance floors and girls wore special – usually silver – dance shoes, which they carried in dolly bags if the weather was inclement. Every girl carried a handbag 'for hanky, gloves and money.' Handbags posed a problem: some were stolen – for little gain – from chairs once dancing had begun and others were deposited in cloakrooms leaving owners with handkerchiefs shoved up sleeves and elastic bands with numbered discs on their wrists. Boys wore their best suits and patent leather shoes called pumps. They perfumed themselves with 4711 or Pershana after-shave and slicked back their hair with Brilliantine or Brylcream.

Most youngsters learned to dance just by going or by watching older brothers and sisters dance to gramophone music in the front rooms. Some older Norwood boys were taught to dance. Several of the Burton Menswear shops had dancehalls above them where couples could practise dancing. Victor Sylvester published a book of dance steps that were drawn as diagrams, and Arthur Murray dance schools boasted the motto 'Dance in a Hurry with Arthur Murray.' A man told us that he paid for dance lessons at a studio but when another man approached him as a potential dance partner, he fled the place in fright and never returned. Although some parents disapproved of dancing, they did concede that it was a way of meeting members of the opposite sex.

Girls sat around the perimeter of the dance floor waiting to hear the words 'Are you dancing?' To which, they replied, 'Are you ask-ing? Then I'm dancing!' and the fun began. The waltz was the first dance anybody learned and good dancers – irrespective of looks, colour or creed – were most often seen on the dance floor. A man joked that although being clubfooted, he danced with the lady of his dreams. When he requested another dance, she refused, accus-ing him of being the worst dancer she had ever seen. His quick retort was, 'What do you want for 2s 6d? Fred Astaire?' It has to be said that 'dancing boys – good dancers, who knew it' did not necessarily make good husbands and girls responded better to the gentlemen – who were in the majority – who ensured their partnership for the last dance, escorted them home, and were satisfied with just a kiss or handshake as a reward.

There were special dances during the evening and a master of ceremonies was in charge. The ladies' 'excuse me' dance gave ladies the opportunity to tap the man of their fancy on the shoulder – whether or not he was partnering someone else at the time – and ask him to dance. Needless to say, the good-looking men or skilled dancers were most in demand. The 'spot dance' meant that a spotlight picked out a dancing couple; who won as a prize a box of chocolates or a vase. Girls seldom danced together – although it was considered acceptable for 'old women to dance together at weddings' – and tall girls were embarrassed to dance with short men lest they 'come up to their bosom.' Few children ever saw their parents dance together. Married men who could not dance at all were taught by their wives to 'shuffle around dance floors' when appropriate. A married couple told us that they had continued to dance together regularly until parental pressure forced them off the dance floor – 'married dancing in public was not nice.' Tea dances where tea, cakes and sandwiches were served were very popular. During the War, two young WAAFs (members of the Women's Auxiliary Air Force) – one a dressmaker and the other a designer – were billeted onto a wealthy household, who rewarded them with a visit to a tea dance because they had made the daughter's wedding dress. However, the unfortunate houseguests were not from 'the right class,' so no one served or danced with them. They were miserable. Wartime dances were regularly held at Covent Garden Opera House. The 'second dance session' from 12.30 a.m. till 4.30 a.m. was particularly popular as famous bands from 'posh' hotels, such as the Savoy, often went on to perform there until the early hours of the morning. American servicemen introduced the Jitterbug dance to their English counterparts and wartime dancing became as sexy and racy as it had been in the 1920s when the Charleston and Black Bottom were in vogue. American soldiers – 'oversexed and over here' – were popular with the ladies. Their uniforms were superior in quality and 'they could offer a girl cigarettes, chocolates and nylon stockings.' A lady told us that she met a soldier at a wartime dance who bought her four drinks. Only after she had gulped them down did she realise they were alcoholic. The poor lady 'danced madly at first' and then fell down onto the floor. Before the War, men seldom bought girls alcoholic drinks – 'people were more innocent then.' They did, however, buy a round of drinks for the band when special requests had been played. A trumpeter who drank too much once asked to lead the band in the National Anthem which was always played at a dance's end. As he stood up to play, he fell off the stage in a drunken heap, leaving his fellow musicians to maintain decorum!

Not everybody danced, of course. One man told us that he read Marx and Engels at a library, which provided him with the peace that his overcrowded home so sadly lacked. Other people preferred playing sport. A lady told us that her boyfriend had reluctantly partnered her on the dance floor only because she had made tea for the players in his cricket team. For a sizeable minority, card games like pontoon, solo, club yosh or 21, were popular and gambling on the horses or dogs – which often worked to the detriment of family life – was compulsive. People watched street entertainers – who hoped for money but did not always receive it – and outdoor debates at Speakers' Corner in Hyde Park that often led to heated discussion. Although there were a number of Jewish pub landlords, few Jews drank. Eating was extremely important. Food was eaten on streets; on outings to the country; in the cinema; and, most luxuriously, in Lyons Corner Houses where you could go for an egg mayonnaise or egg and chips.

The Yiddish Theatre where the plays performed – although mainly comedies – always met audiences' requirements for 'a good cry', and in the Music Halls, where poor performers were sometimes fished off the stage with a hook wielded by the manager, were good places to let off steam.

Visits to the cinema – called 'flicks' or 'pictures' – were sources of excitement and active participation. Even when seated before silent screens, audiences cheered their heroes and cried 'look behind you' to warn away villains. Cinemas were either 'fleapits' furnished with benches where usherettes regularly sprayed both floor and audience with insect repellent, or more comfortable establishments with padded single seats and dual seats for courting couples in the back rows. When films broke down in either type of cinema, and this they frequently did, audiences whistled and catcalled until service was resumed – albeit in the form of a 'flicker,'

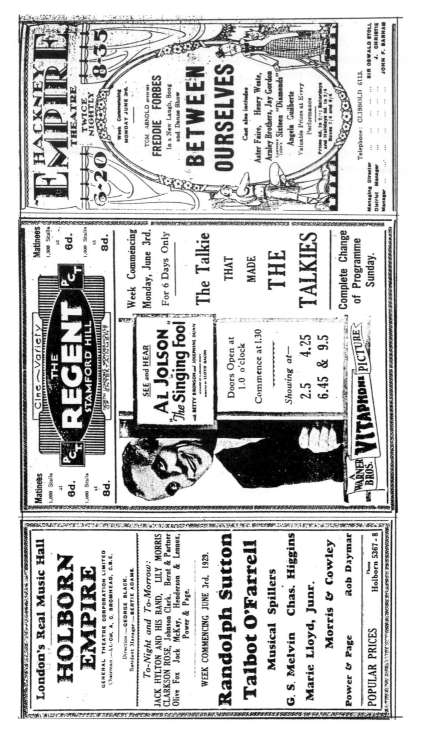

36. An advertisement for the Holborn Empire, The Regent at Stamford Hill, and the Hackney Empire Theatre, shows the wide range of entertainment available in the late 1920s. *North London Recorder*, 31 May 1929. [Courtesy of the British Museum Newspaper Library, Colindale.]

that is, a picture flicking up and down on the screen. Films, which were changed once or twice weekly, were silent until the 1930s. Jewish cinemagoers who could not read English subtitles sometimes paid children to accompany them as translators. Audience members who lacked this advantage either craned their necks to catch the Yiddish – and were reprimanded for so doing – or loudly berated the children for disrupting. Cinema-going was far from passive! Luxurious cinemas – like the Astoria, Finsbury Park, which boasted a tearoom, a goldfish pool and a ceiling which resembled a starry sky, and the Troxy, which accommodated as many as 3,000 people and presented *King Kong* starring Fay Wray at its first-ever showing – showed two films, an 'A' and then a 'B.' The B film showed first and often 'starred second-rate actors such as Ronald Reagan.' Pathé News – for some, the only source of connection to the outside world – usually opened the proceedings. Some cinemas staged variety shows between the A and B films and first-rate performers often appeared on stage. Audiences formed lengthy queues on the pavements outside, at the box office, and in the aisles of the cinema, before the entertainment began. Street entertainers and buskers sometimes kept the waiting public amused. A lady remembered seeing an escapologist who was so inept at his craft, that he remained in chains – and unpaid – long after the queues had dissipated. A pianist who adapted his/her playing to the pace of the film always accompanied the silent movies and, at a later date, an organist, poised at an organ that rose dramatically out of the floor, played in between the films. Films showed continuously at local cinemas – which were abundant. If anyone missed the start of a film, they waited until it came around again to catch it – and then left. Films were given ratings and 'H' stood for horror; no children were admitted. If there were bedroom scenes, stars had to keep one foot on the floor and 'kissing was as far as it went.'

Children sometimes sneaked into forbidden performances through toilet windows or fire escapes. If caught at all, they were lifted up by the scruff of the neck, evicted and advised to stick to children's programmes that were shown on Saturday mornings, or to matinee performances known as 'the tupenny rush.' A man told us that his wife kicked her high-heeled shoes off while seated in the cinema. Because the lady's feet swelled up during the screening, her shoes no longer fitted her and she had to be carried over floors littered with peanut shells, orange peel, boxes of chocolates and newspaper to the safety of the pavement outside. Like dancing, the 'flicks' provided an escape from the humdrum. Women with large families found peace and quiet in the cinema and a fantasy life along with the movie stars. In the silent movie era, serial films were shown and audiences would return to see heroes untie heroines from railway lines 'just in the nick of time.' In the 1920s and 1930s ladies wore large hats to the cinema which – although challenging to other members of the audience – presented less of a problem than the beehive hairstyles of the 1950s which 'could not be taken off.' If youngsters arrived late for a 'showing' they often stood up before the screen in the hope that their friends might spot them. Whatever the chaos, the National Anthem gathered all – or, at least, those who had not rushed out first – together at the evening's end. 'Even anarchists and communists stood still with respect.' People then spilled outside to buy fish and chips, jacket potatoes or other delicacies from stalls on the street.

37. Harry Finn in the Norwood JLB band, 1926.

For the younger members of the community, youth clubs provided entertainment, sport, culture and, for some, a place of refuge. These clubs were initially set up before the First World War by wealthy Jewish benefactors – like the Rothschild, Goldsmid, Montagu, Mocatta and Rufus Isaacs families – who were anxious to Anglicise and integrate the mainly Russian-Jewish immigrant population into British society as quickly as possible. Later on, it was hoped that the youth clubs would keep young boys out of trouble and away from the gambling dens so prevalent between the Wars. The popular East End Clubs were the JLB (Jewish Lads' Brigade), which had a brass band and rifle range; the Brady Boys' Club; the Oxford and St George's, which encouraged boxing; and the Victoria Working Boys' Club. The West Central was the only West End Boys' Club; and the Mile End Old Boys' Club was set up to meet older boys' needs. These clubs encouraged participation in sporting activities, arranged holidays, and tried to raise members' aspirations by introducing them to classical music and drama. Girls' clubs were set up later than boys' clubs and were not, on the

38. The Oxford and St George's Club in Berner Street, E1, was one of the many youth clubs set up with the intent of keeping young boys off the streets. This is a postcard addressed to Mrs Phillips in Orchid Road, N14, showing (back row) Jack R., Ben A., Jack G., R.W., and Scholy; (front row) Willie S., Ike G., M.O.S., Alf G., and Ben D.

whole, as well attended. Girls had classes in personal hygiene, and needlework and housewifery, and were also introduced to the classics. Lily Montague would invite girls from the West Central Club to her house for tea. The girls were expected to behave with appropriate decorum. At the Settlement Club, Lady Henriques did not allow the girls to use some of the staircases for fear that boys might 'look up their skirts.'

Youth clubs played a major part in the lives of Jewish youth until the Second World War. Youth leaders were usually well-spoken and regarded as a race apart, and the youngsters did try to emulate their speech and dress. They strove very hard to teach comradeship, teamwork and responsibility, and to expose the young members to a different world. Some clubs encouraged political discussion, some were simply rambling clubs, and others taught children elocution and ways of putting their own lyrics to popular operatic songs. Most of the clubs ran camping holidays that were eagerly anticipated, and which afforded many children an escape from cramped living conditions – not to mention a first sighting of the countryside or the sea. Many people remembered the showers which were just 'buckets of water tipped over you' and the soap, which they brought home 'still wrapped' as a souvenir.

As children became adults and memories of youthful excursions remained, they incorporated outings to the sea and the country-side, or visits to parks, into their leisure calendar. The most pop-ular venues were Southend, where the pier was considered 'com-mon,' and Westcliff, which was 'posher.' Travelling to Southend and back on a Saturday evening was an easy option. You caught the six o'clock train, watched a band playing in a local hotel, and were back by midnight – all for a shilling return! Margate, which was 'less Jewish' than nearby Cliftonville, was another favourite destination. Days out were taken seriously. Many men wore jackets and ties for the occasion and women, summer frocks with jackets. The more modern in the community wore one-piece bathing suits or generous trunks, and bald men covered their heads with hand-kerchiefs tied in knots at the four corners. When the tide was out, you could see men in their jackets, ties and rolled-up trouser legs walking across the mud. Women waded out to paddle with their

My dear friends,

I am writing this to you, dear Club members, as my message to you when I pass away. G-d has given us the power to love and so we will never be really separated, as love is eternal.

I have been most happy serving with you and for you. I began work when I was a girl of 18 and have found that work brings a great deal of happiness through friendship which is the best of all blessings. Although I had no previous training in social work, I think I began on the right lines. Its main object was to make the Club members develop their capabilities and to learn to serve each other. Through our love of G-d we are able to serve his Children. I am glad that through the Club some of you have learned to appreciate and discover the true meaning of JUDAISM. Do try and cling to your faith and live by it, and express it in your lives.

Then I have tried to bring before you a high ideal of friendship and of continued education. The Club classes have given you a wider outlook and opportunities for relaxation. I have endeavoured during my Club life to show you the things that are eternal, I don't accept anything that is cheap or vulgar. Remember that you must respect your womanhood and manhood, never cheapen it by loose living, you life comes from

G-d, live so that when your time comes you will have made your corner of the world a little better than you found it. You must guard the highest ideal of Jewish womanhood and manhood.

Now dear friends, make your membership worthy of the Club, give of your best to it and to one another. Remember that G-d can be found at all times, and behave as if you were in His presence. Let our Club be a Jewish Club because only the best will be found there, that Judaism and its teachings will be appreciated and lived by, otherwise why a Jewish Club?

Finally, I would ask you to make our Club a happy place, a place of peace and hope, wherein happiness can be sanctified and sorrow softened through friendship.

And now, dear children, goodbye and G-d bless you and help you in all you try to do. I know you won't forget your Club mother very quickly; she loves you all and will continue to do so from her new home. She leaves you her work unfinished and very imperfect so that you can complete and improve it.

Your affectionate friend and Club mother
LILY H. MONTAGU

39. **The strong moral and religious purposes behind youth clubs is made clear in this letter from Lily Montagu (d. 22 January 1963). This letter was found after her death and was addressed to her club members. [Courtesy of Mrs Nellie G. Levy.]**

40. A 'charabanc' outing to Westcliffe. Everyone sat in the square overlooking the sea by the toilets opposite the tea stall, *not* on the beach. [Courtesy of Freda Stanton.]

MARGATE
HOTEL SPLENDIDE, Cliftonville

IS NOW OPEN   Early Application Essential
REDUCED TERMS FOR JUNE AND JULY

Largest and most luxuriously furnished Jewish Hotel in the United Kingdom; facing tennis courts and overlooking sea; over 50 bedrooms, fitted hot and cold water, gas fires, etc.; magnificent dining room, spacious lounge, ball-room, smoke room, ladies' drawing room; excellent cuisine; licensed for wines; garage accommodation; open to non-residents.

Illustrated Tariff on Application.

A. WESTRICH, Proprietor

Telegrams: "Hotel Splendide, Margate."   Telephone: Margate 300.

---

41. An advertisement from the 1930s for the 'most luxuriously furnished Jewish Hotel in the United Kingdom'. [Courtesy of the British Museum Newspaper Library, Colindale.]

skirts tucked into their bloomers. When the tide came in, rows of deck chairs moved away from beach onto the promenade, where, in Margate particularly, photographers often photographed people holding stuffed animals like bears or tigers, and donkey rides or

Punch and Judy shows entertained the crowds. A man remembered his father taking a cake of soap to the seaside so that his
family could 'wash themselves in the sea' and another remembered the thrill of meeting James Woolf, the first Jewish swimmer
to cross the English Channel. In Westcliff, Jewish holidaymakers
chose to congregate around the promenade rather than sit near
the pier so that they could gossip there with friends and neighbours. The 'oval' bandstand at Cliftonville was a popular meeting
point. A postcard sent home with the message 'having a good time'
was *de rigueur* for those whose seaside sojourns lasted more than
a few days.

There were many Jewish boarding houses like Mrs Apfel's in
Cliftonville and most are remembered as strict establishments.
Boarding houses charged about 30s a week, never served lunch,
and expected guests to abide by their rules. Supper was served
promptly at 5.30 p.m.; there was no choice of food and guests
were expected to be punctual. One lady remembered seeing a
maggot in the chicken served to her from a boarding house
kitchen. When she complained, the owner replied, 'No one else
has complained – so eat it!' During the day – and even if it was
raining – guests had to vacate the boarding houses until supper

42. Ann and Sam Boxer enjoy a day at the seaside. Note the attire!

95

was served. This meant that Lyons Tea Houses, teashops and cinemas did a roaring trade. Not everyone was lucky enough to be able to afford this. Most people took picnics with them from home and these might include boiled egg sandwiches, pickled cucumber, herrings, *cholent*, and chicken legs. Those with cars took deck-chairs and card tables. Food was supplemented with cups of tea bought from seaside stalls. When seaside holidays ended, people returned home refreshed and 'looking like beetroots.'

Days spent in the countryside or in local parks were also popular. Box Hill, Clissold Park in Stoke Newington, Springfield Park in Clapton and Victoria Park were favoured venues. People went for boat rides on lakes, played cricket or football and men – wearing jackets and ties – sometimes impressed ladies with their rowing skills. A man told us that he took his wife punting from Twicken-ham to Richmond, paid ten shilllings for the privilege and spent a blissful evening 'canoodling' in private. This romantic activity sometimes took place on coach trips and trains where the maxi-mum speed was 30 miles per hour. The moonlight often seen through windows on evening excursions – by those not otherwise engaged, of course – brought to mind the Frankie Vaughan song, 'Give me the Moonlight.'

Whatever the chosen escape route, people returned to their daily routines with a fresh perspective. There was one leisure activity which coloured everybody's life – wherever they were – and that was eating!

Living to Eat

The 1930s' larder was a curious mixture of a 'preserve and con-serve' or 'just in case' culture and the practical recognition that there was no need to waste precious money by storing anything but staples and basic foods. This was despite the fact that the Jew-ish mother was providing meals and snacks for husband and chil-dren up to five or six times a day – 'We did not hoard food, we made it fresh'; 'Jewish families seemed to eat on demand!'

Without refrigeration, food did not keep fresh for long and it was just as well that there were shops on every corner, markets no more than five minutes walk away, and a local dairy such as Evans on nearly every street. It was but a short distance to pop out several times a day, if necessary, to buy a pat of butter, a jug of milk, a few eggs, or, for special occasions, a 'tonce' (two ounces) of smoked salmon. Because storage was a luxury and money scarce, goods were often put on 'tick' and the bill settled on payday.

Larders were smaller than the ones we know today, and the typical contents of a pre-war Jewish larder might include the following staples: acetic acid – malt vinegar or Sarcens vinegar; lump sugar – especially if you were Polish or Russian – for serv-ing with lemon tea; Nestle's tinned condensed milk; Camp liquid coffee – mixed with chicory; *pflaumen*, that is, prunes or other dried fruit such as apricots and apples; Libby's tinned peaches; Del Monte's tinned fruit; haricot beans; butter beans; lentils; a block or brick of salt, kept in a tin or earthenware jar with a *reebazen* (grater) for koshering meat; *lum dust* (granulated sugar); loose tea in packets – such as Brook Bond, Liptons, J. Lyons and Co. (twopence a pack) and Mazawatee; porridge – Quaker Oats, bought loose in bags; Rakusens/Bonds matzo meal; nuts – such as hazelnuts; sacks of rice from the Port of London Author- ity – especially in households of Sephardic origin; preserves and pickles – all homemade, of course; jams, which were often quite exotic like carrot jam, rhubarb and ginger jam, or marmalade; pickled onions; *chrayne* – white horseradish with added beetroot; pickled cucumber; pickled red cabbage; sauerkraut; pickled her- ring – a dozen herrings for pickling cost one shilling; a jar of *schmaltz* – chicken fat for chopped liver and *grieven* (deep-fried chicken fat); *lockshen* – noodles, homemade on Thursday for *Shabbat*; cherry brandy; raisin wine; and, very occasionally, Lyons products for emergencies. There were no tinned vegetables, no packaged biscuits, very little colour, and, of course, no plastic wrapping.

Most households had a safe, which was a small box with a mesh front door that allowed air to circulate and kept food fresh. As a rule, the safe usually placed outside the kitchen window, on the balcony, or in the back yard. People remember butter, cheese and milk stored in jugs, or left-over meat, freshly cooked tongues left to cool, and chicken soup being stored in the safe. Most freshly cooked food was covered with muslin – available from John Lewis for 6d a yard and sometimes decorated with beads to weigh down the corners.

'Preserving and conserving' always taxed the housewife's ingenuity and it was required of her that she be extremely inventive. A lady remembered her mother's jellied carp or calf's foot jelly always cooling down on the cold stone kitchen floor; onions and other vegetables were removed from chicken soup left warming on the stove lest they 'turn it;' and milk, bought – often more than once daily – from milkmen's churns, the dairy or corner shop, was 'boiled again at home' in warm weather before being stored in jugs. 'Nothing was ever wasted' and there was always something to eat. For example, if milk was left out, it was allowed to go sour on a

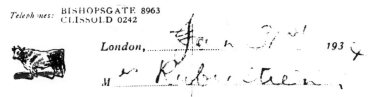

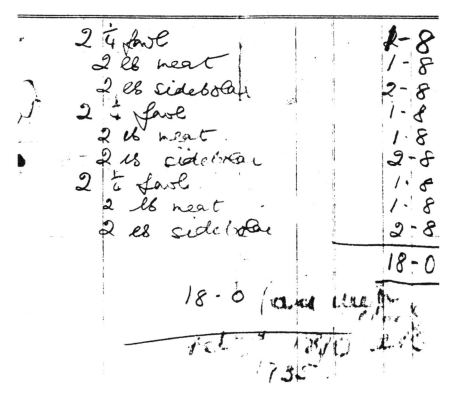

43. Although shops were frequently close to home many, such as S. Waterman & Sons, would deliver orders to your door.

window ledge and then dripped through a muslin bag held over the sink to make sour milk or cream cheese. One man spoke with pride of his 'Ma's kitchen range' which 'always had a pot of coffee on the stove, jacket potatoes in the oven and a *wurst* in the drawer.'

99

Fruit and vegetables, which were mainly English and available only 'in season,' were hardly ever stored, as the housewife bought them daily. If it was the season for runner beans, then you had runner beans. In season there were English strawberries, black-berries, medlars (a type of soft apple), and 'cos' lettuce (one penny a lettuce from a market barrow).

A typical day's catering for the busy housewife might go as follows:

- Breakfast: porridge, bread and butter, jam, bagel, cream cheese, eggs.
- Lunch for school children: this usually included soup – such as borscht, cabbage soup or barley soup with dumplings.
- After-school snack: a slice of black bread and *schmaltz* or *grieven*; or milk and homemade biscuits like *kirchels* or cake: homemade, of course!
- Later in the day, she prepared dinner for her children and the same, again, for her husband.

Mother's industry did not stop at this. There was still the endless variety of dishes to cook and prepare for Jewish holidays and special times!

Although providing sensible meals at home was the all-consuming, top priority for women in charge of the household, eating for pleasure or 'noshing' outside the home was rapidly becoming a popular pastime with new generations – after dancing and going to the 'flicks.' Much depended on the money in your pockets. Young children might spend pocket money, which varied according to circumstances from a farthing a day up to about 6 d a week, or money earned from doing odd jobs, on snacks such as crisps in bags 'with blue salt packets,' cones of broken biscuits bought from the grocer, or bits from the bottom of the chip pan called 'crackling,' which were sold in bags and were 'cheaper than chips.' Favourite of all, were sweets, of course, and the best of these included Acid Drops, Lucky Dips (that 'had surprises inside'), Sherbet Dabs, Swizz Sticks, Bulls Eyes, Brandy Balls, Aniseed Balls, Gobstoppers (that changed colour in your mouth), pink and white Coconut Squares, Toshes Liquorice (that came in cartwheel, twig or lace form), and cough sweets called **Paregoric Sweets** (that were orange and strong-tasting). Moishe Taster, the toffee vendor, chopped up pieces of treacle-, seed- or palm-toffee; and, for special treats, children could buy Rowntree's **Walnut Whipped Creams** for two and a half pence each. Sweetshops were usually small and cramped and sold cigarettes, ice cream, and lemonade or 'sasparella' to drink, as well as sweets. Sweets were kept in big glass jars out of children's reach and were weighed out on scales as required. Some local shops made their own sweets and shops, such as the Mikado Sweetshop in Aldgate, usually opened at eight in the morning and stayed open until eight at night. Some children secretly spent bus- or tram-fare money on sweets – even if it meant having to walk to school and back – and it was the height of every child's ambition to own a sweet shop. A lady said, 'You may think we were greedy, but most of us ate sweets only once a day and simply spent our farthings and half-pennies.'

A penny went a long way. For only one penny you could buy chips – 'a penn'orth of chips and vinegar from Johnny Isaacs,' a pick-led cucumber from Mossy Marks in the Lane [Petticoat Lane] or a jacket potato from a stall. Assenheim's in Finch Street sold ice cream cones; half a penny for the wafer and a penny for the ice cream – white or pink. Their advertisement went, 'Hokey pokey, penny a lump, the more you eat, the more you jump!' Arrowroot biscuits – 'Oh, so fine and sweet' – cost a penny; broken biscuits bought either in a paper cone from the grocer or direct from the Meredith and Drew factory cost a penny; and a slice of water-melon in season, an apple or 'three lemons to suck' cost the same. Marks and Spencer started out as a 'penny bazaar,' and Woolworth once sold nothing over a penny.

Teenagers with a bit of money in their pockets – especially when dressed up to go out on Saturday nights – might buy more sub-stantial snacks like fish and chips; herrings wrapped in news-paper; 'boxer' or locust fruit (a type of dried up black banana-shaped fruit with seeds and a sweet taste); or tiger nuts, polish nuts or monkey nuts, the shells of which were littered all over cinema floors after performances. There were no ready prepared sandwiches available, but you could buy hot cross buns, muffins and currant buns from the street seller or bagels from Esther – four for a penny or five for tuppence: 'Bagels, bagels for the Duke of York, if you don't want them, you can go for a walk.'

Young wage earners splashed out on tea dances and restaurants. Most famous of these were the Lyons Tea Houses and Corner Houses, started by Montague Gluckstein and Joseph Lyons. There

44. Lyons were the most famous tea houses in London. [Courtesy of the British Museum Newspaper Library, Colindale.]

were four Corner Houses: one in Coventry Road, one at Marble Arch, one in the Strand, and one in Leicester Square. The Corner Houses were considered to be 'very posh;' there were tablecloths on the tables and waitress service. 'When you went to the Corner House you felt like a film star because someone waited on you and the china all matched and the tea was in a tea pot, the milk in a jug and the sugar in a bowl.' This was not to mention the cutlery, much admired and sometimes pilfered by customers! 'Egg mayonnaise' was a Corner House speciality and it was said that 'Nobody made egg mayonnaise like the Corner House.' A man said that the waitresses – called 'Nippies' because they dashed around

Phone: ROYAL 6450.

London, November 1, 1906

Mr. Sheinman

ESTIMATE FROM SCHWARTZ,

כשר Restaurant. כשר

5. 6 & 7. ALDGATE EAST CHAMBERS.
(Facing Aldgate East Station.)

WEDDINGS, BANQUETS, Etc., CATERED IN SUPERIOR STYLE.

45 couples @ 12/- - - - £27 . 0 . 0

To extras for Refreshments ...   £ . 0 . 0

(as arranged with Mr Sheinman)

To Refreshments for Band of 3.   12 . 0 .
@ 4/- per head.

£31   12 . 0

Deposit   2 .   0 . 0

Balance £29 .   12 . 0

Received with thanks.

£29 . 12 . 0

S. Schwartz

45. Kosher restaurants could be hired out for weddings.

serving people – would joke with Jewish customers, particularly, 'I suppose you want two egg mayonnaise,' before menus had even been provided. Some of the Corner Houses had orchestras and people dressed up in their best suits and ties or frocks to go there.

Other favoured eating venues included the ABC (Aerated Bread Company) chain of shops 'which were not as good as Lyons,' and Blooms, where it was rumoured that the waiters had stop watches and allowed customers only 15 minutes' seating time. Kosher restaurants, such as Goides, could be hired out for weddings. It was quite usual for staff to line up outside the door at the end of the evening with their hands held out for gratuities, reminding you that they had 'peeled the potatoes for your dinner.' Johnny Isaacs on the Mile End Road, and Sacks and Fat Annie on Vallance Road, served the best fish and chips and, for afternoon tea, you went to Wyckhams which served 'lovely cream buns' or Zimmerman's, facing Spitalfields Market in Commercial Road, where 'all the *frummers*' went. The more affluent in the community could go to tea dances at the Ritz, which served egg or cucumber sandwiches. After the War, so-called 'black and white milk bars' served coffee and milk shakes: a favourite of these bars was called 'The Moo Cow.'

Parents hardly ever ate outside of their homes, except when they attended weddings and other such celebrations; on the whole, they left this leisure activity to the young. 'We had a few bob in our pockets and we spent it on food;' 'We would travel up West on a Saturday, see a film and then go to Lyons Corner House for a nosh;' 'We were the first generation to break out into the outside world;' 'We were with it, we wanted everything: dancing, films, food.' This was the first generation of 'noshers' outside the home and, as such, they were pioneers.

The Value of Remembering the Past

For some people, the brush of advancing years paints a rosy glow on the past, but for others their past remains a place of sadness and deprivation. Many feel proud to have survived at all, but some are sad not to have experienced the advantages of educational opportunity. Some feel honoured to have contributed to, while others are glad to have escaped from, their communities. Some regard the family as a source of nourishment while others remember it as a place of pain. Some lived life to the full – whatever their financial situation – while others, unfortunately, were too limited by circumstances to break away. In whatever way they lived, these men and women have one thing in common: they are the witnesses of yesterday, survivors of a former age.

Most people are proud to be able to recall incidents from their past: 'Each one of us can remember a different shop or place;' 'I did not realise how much I could remember;' 'This warms our hearts;' 'It is amazing how we can recall incidents – even 80 years ago.' Just imagine, for instance, there were no sirens during the First World War and a solitary policeman on his bicycle had to urgently blow his whistle to warn the community of approaching Zeppelin airships! Compare our computer age to the time when houses were lit by gaslight or candles. Members of the community could stroll down streets peopled with gossiping housewives, tradesmen, entertainers, or children at play. Most people remember having to do as their parents told them, having to listen to and respect the old and to learn from their wisdom. Some spoke of leaving school at 13 or 14 to go to work in sweatshops, and others of sharing beds with several siblings – which discomfort made them 'less squeamish and more tolerant.' Some recalled the *vanzen* – the 'red army' – the plague of their times. Many remembered the inconvenience of mother's 'home remedies' (administered with love, of course), like having to wear a sock round the neck if suffering from a sore throat or having to place horse manure on swollen knees. Children of compulsive gamblers learned the hard way to save their own money, or, at the least, to spend it wisely. Most learned to manage on pitifully little. The pace of life was slower and the community spirit stronger. 'We lived together in small communities, like ghettoes in the big cities.' 'We were never lonely because we were always surrounded by people with similar problems.' 'It was a golden age.' 'We were all one.' There were street parties held on public holidays and communal rejoicing at individual good news. People visited cinemas, dance halls and the seaside to get 'away from it all.' Most remembered shared loss, the rituals of courtship, and the community's involvement in their wedding preparations. People spoke of their poverty and hunger in the time of Stanley Baldwin and of their fortitude in the face of Moseley's Fascist marches. They remembered being told that 'British' was always best.

People said that moral codes were clearer, differences between 'right' and 'wrong' more defined, and the messages youth received less confused than those of today. 'We could not always do what we wanted, but that was a good thing.' Children were taught to 'live a clean life,' 'leave a good name,' and that 'work is the foundation of good health.' The War, however, altered everything. Houses, families, whole streets, were destroyed. The East End community, once a source of shelter, became too confining; women's housewifery, once revered, too restricting; the lack of contact with other lifestyles, too limiting; the old ways, no longer appropriate. 'We are the first survivors of this modern age but, in all the confusion, we simply lived to rebuild our lives. We did not prepare for old age: we did not expect to live this long.'

Like gathering up autumn leaves lying dormant under a tree, reminiscence revives these lost memories and gives them colour.

Old people have the opportunity, through talking and discussing, to re-evaluate their lives and reflect on the gains and losses of their times. Many people say that reminiscing makes them feel wanted, gives them a sense of belonging and dignity and diminishes their loneliness. Reminiscence is in the natural order of things: through it, the old can enjoy and relive so much that has gone past while we, the listeners, hope, in turn, to be able to pass their stories on to our young. Most of all, perhaps, the threads of our social history are kept strong. The witnesses of yesterday are messengers for tomorrow. By hearing their tales we keep our cultural heritage alive.

Our project brought us much joy and enriched our lives. It could have worked in any community where old and young can share experiences. We found that there were unexpected benefits: old

46. Reminiscence groups provide a valuable opportunity for the old and young to share their experiences. [Courtesy of City of London Girls School.]

friends were reunited in the groups and long-lost family members found. Barriers were broken down between generations, lives validated, wounds healed and problems solved. 'We are like one big family;' 'There is something of worth in everybody;' 'We get recognition;' 'We might not have a future, but we have had a past;' 'I am 93 years old. When I look back I realise how much I have seen, and I want to share it.' 'Talking about the past is like applying paint to a blank canvas' – and therein lies the value of reminiscence.

How to Reminisce: A Practical Guide

As the previous chapters have shown, a wealth of unique and priceless information can be revived through our reminiscence sessions. Stories, personalities and details of life increase our understanding of the social history of previous generations.

Over the last ten years we have developed a number of ways of training people to run reminiscence groups. We have also used reminiscence to enhance communication with very frail or confused people who would find it difficult to participate in a group.

Training sessions include discussion about the value of reminiscence, the role of the group leader, and the use of memorabilia. In these sessions the volunteers and care staff learn to structure a reminiscence session, to trigger memory, to draw out information, to build self-esteem and to create a warm and trusting environment. Such sessions can last from a few hours to a full day. Participants are given the opportunity to exchange memories on topics such as songs remembered from childhood or favourite outfits. When volunteers offer their own stories and share their feelings, ice is broken between strangers. People come to understand themselves, each other and a group dynamic. Group leaders come to understand participants.

How to begin?
BE PRACTICAL. BE POSITIVE. BE PREPARED.
When a new group is being planned this needs to be advertised. Leaflets are not enough. People – whether in a community centre

or residential home – need to be wooed and encouraged into com-ing along. If they don't know what reminiscence is, they may need to be reassured that they don't have to talk if they would prefer to remain silent. The layout of the room is important. It should be an enclosed space with no outside distractions. A group of chairs brought into as small a circle as possible enables group members to hear, see and share easily – and an atmosphere of intimacy is created.

The group should be planned to take place during mid-morning or mid-afternoon so that members are alert – not too hungry and not longing for a snooze after a pleasant meal. The optimum length of a session is about 45 minutes to an hour. In the case of people with dementia who have very short concentration spans about ten minutes is sufficient. The aim is to create a special time, a special place, a special atmosphere. Regularity and commitment build up the trust and credibility of a group.

47. **Members of the North East London Day Centre Stamford Hill in the Reminiscence Room.**

GROUP SIZE?

Flexibility is the keynote here. It is important to stress that groups can range from two to 30 depending on the setting and the type of people you are working with. In a community centre where the people are alert and articulate 8–15 would be the optimum number. Where people are suffering from dementia, working with two people or on a one-to-one basis is more worthwhile. It is not the numbers that matter. If the memories evoked produce enjoyment, a feeling of self-esteem and recognition of each individual's unique past then your aim has been achieved.

WHO REMINISCES?

Any older person can reminisce. Groups are made up of people from all walks of life: taxi drivers, shopkeepers, tailors, housewives and accountants can all enjoy sharing recollections of earlier days. Previous education has no relevance, reminiscence is 'a leveller.' Many older people have a better memory for the past than for the present so reminiscing builds on these strengths. For example, one group found it easier to list in detail the contents of their larders of 60 years ago than those of last week's shopping basket.

If people with dementia, however, are in a group with mentally alert people, the former may feel inadequate and the latter frustrated. It is easier to run a group if all members have a similar capacity to participate.

LEADING A GROUP

It may sound obvious, but creating an atmosphere of warmth and encouragement is vital to the success of any group. It is important to look round the group and notice when someone wants to speak; don't forget the person sitting next to you and do not be deflected if everyone talks at the same time. Use active listening skills. Demonstrate by your body language and by encouraging nods and facial expressions that you are concentrating on what is being said. Encourage active response and cross-group discussion because this will trigger memories of greater depth and breadth.

Ask questions that will draw out information, using the list of questions you have prepared beforehand. At the same time be sen-

111

sitive about not being too intrusive or pressing people to respond when they cannot remember, as this could be counter-productive. The purpose here is to build on strengths.

It is helpful if the person running the group takes notes so that memories can be recorded accurately. Without our notes we could not have written this book. In reminiscence older people are our teachers. So many older people are physically dependent and the recipients of constant help. Reminiscence provides an opportunity for them to give.

WHAT DO WE TALK ABOUT AND HOW DO WE BEGIN?
In our approach, it is essential that the person running the group has an 'action plan' that includes an introduction, a selection of questions and a conclusion. The sessions start off by linking the present with the past. For example, you might say, 'My head is reeling with information from television programmes and newspapers. How did you find out what was going on in the world?' (A number of sample action plans are given in Appendix C). In our training sessions we ask participants to devise their own introductions and lists of questions on particular topics.

TOPIC BOXES
In addition to group discussion there are other creative ways of using memorabilia. At Jewish Care, over 65 topic boxes were created by two volunteers that covered a range of topics – from fashion, transport, and Jewish Festivals, to the Second World War. Action plans are included in each topic box so that group leaders are able to introduce topics and give informed and constructive prompts. Much of the information in these action plans is based on reminiscence groups' recollections gathered over the last 12 years. The topic boxes include photographs, old magazines and newspaper articles, and objects with different smells and textures. Older people's sense of smell is important – mothballs, lavender bags and carbolic soap, for example, can be very evocative.

Each topic should offer fun and enjoyment and enhance self-esteem and, at the same time, enrich the lives of the recipients of these personal and unique memories.

Problems: What to do if...

A GROUP MEMBER IS VISUALLY IMPAIRED?

Remember in the initial planning stages that visually impaired people will not see leaflets advertising the group so be sure to tell them and encourage them to come, reassuring them that the group will be sensitive to their particular needs. Both the person running the group and its members should be aware of the need to describe the objects and photographs being discussed to anyone with a visual impairment.

A GROUP MEMBER IS HARD OF HEARING?

Speak in a low tone of voice that is easier to hear. Make sure that the person can see the movements of your mouth. Ensure that the door is closed so that there are no competing noises nearby. Make sure that the person who is hard of hearing is seated near or next to you. Be prepared to repeat a story if necessary.

A GROUP MEMBER BECOMES DISTRESSED?

Very occasionally it is possible that a particular topic causes a moment of sadness or distress. It is absolutely essential that the person running the group observes the group members carefully and notices any signs of upset. Be sure to give time after the group finishes to see if anyone wants to talk about what might have upset them, and before you leave do mention any upset to the member of staff on duty, or any other appropriate person so that there is an awareness of the problem and vigilance is maintained. If someone shares a sad memory that the group receives sensitively, the outcome could be beneficial.

SOMEONE DOMINATES THE GROUP?

Everyone should have an opportunity to talk if they wish, otherwise an atmosphere of frustration develops. The person running the group needs to maintain an element of control here, although it is important that this is done as tactfully as possible and without in any way disparaging or diminishing the dominating member. It may be that the person running the group will need to emphasise the importance of listening as well as talking. Don't be afraid of being the leader. Someone has to be!

113

SOMEONE MISSES A GROUP SESSION?

Because reminiscence groups create a sense of belonging, it is worth contacting the member concerned to see if he/she is all right and to welcome him/her back after a period of absence.

Reminiscence with people with dementia

People with dementia respond more effectively on a one-to-one basis or in very small groups of preferably not more than two or three.

Find out as much as you can about their past – from relatives, for example – so that you can ask relevant questions. Develop an individual reminiscence profile, for example, date of birth, key life events, and so on. Base reminiscence on these events. It is no good asking people about the East End of London if they were born in Manchester!

Reminisce for short spells only – perhaps five or ten minutes – as people with dementia have short concentration spans. Be aware of the fact that they can have as many periods when they are quite lucid and articulate as when they are quite confused, and in the same day. Seize the moment when an opportunity arises, perhaps at meal times or bath times. It is not necessary to have a formal time to reminisce. It is important to be sensitive to mood and mental state when deciding on the time to reminisce. Be prepared to go over the same ground more than once and be flexible about pace, giving the person time to absorb the question and respond in whatever way they are able. If they are not responding gently repeat the question using slightly different words, in case, perhaps, you have not been understood or the question forgotten. Do watch for non-verbal reactions; these can be very significant. A slight nod of the head, a tear or a smile can indicate a response and communication at some level. It is necessary to be realistic about what can be achieved in order that you should not feel discouraged. Holding the attention of a very confused person for even one minute is a real achievement.

Don't press people with dementia to answer questions as this can produce lowered self-esteem and increase anxiety. Offer a comment yourself, or gently change the subject.

Stimulate as many senses as possible. As mentioned before, smells can be evocative and photographs of family events can be helpful in triggering memories. The most important trigger for people with dementia is that of music. It is often very rewarding and moving to see people who have very little short-term memory singing the words of an old song, or recalling the words of a once significant religious song, such as 'Kol Nidre' that is sung on the Day of Atonement.

What are we aiming for?

FOR THE CARER?

Reminiscence brings carers closer to the people they are looking after. It gives them an understanding of an individual's past that may provide clues to their present-day personality. In cases where the carer is a family member it can be beneficial to both parties to recall memories of happier times.

FOR THE YOUNGER PERSON?

The passing on of our cultural heritage is an important part of reminiscence. These people are witnesses of yesterday and can offer children primary historical evidence. Our particular programme provides current and future generations with detailed information about the lives and attitudes of the Jewish community in

48. Reminiscence groups can be an important source of information for the young on their community's cultural heritage. [Courtesy of City of London Girls School.]

115

London in the first half of the twentieth century. Many of the volunteers involved in our reminiscence work are middle aged. They learn about their heritage in a way they might not have done from their own parents and grandparents.

Fun and laughter. A sense of enjoyment is intrinsically invaluable and beneficial to health. Reminiscence also stimulates memory and encourages people to focus their minds and to concentrate. People grow in self-esteem and often visibly blossom when recapturing memories of their families or working lives. 'Talking about the olden days made me realise how much I have achieved during my life,' a group member said. Successful reminiscence groups can also create feelings of belonging and mutual respect.

Learning how to reminisce is like gaining a skill that allows the elderly to recall details that are lost forever – sorrow, joy, and ordinary humdrum days. Reminiscence brings self-esteem, enjoyment, knowledge and delight to all those associated with it. It enriches and can even prolong their lives.

In the words of one of our members:

On Growing Old

We should not dread the thought of growing old.
Regard it as an end to be achieved.
Of youth's trite problems we shall be relieved.
While oft times age can bring us joys untold.

Though there is much we can no longer do,
Since ageing limbs our efforts soon prevent,
Yet can that hour to us be Heaven sent.
There are so many aims we can pursue.

To sit at ease and watch the world go by,
To muse upon the years now far behind,
The memory of one's friends to bring to mind,
Relive our life in dreams, we tend to try.

And when we thus look back upon times past,
Recalling all the stresses and the strains
That we have undergone, the growing pains
Of living out our life, and then we cast

An eye on what the future holds in store.
Old we may be in years, but young at heart.
Thus ageing gracefully, we play our part.
So much there is that is worth living for.

Solomon Leff

Appendix A
A *Yiddishe* Winkel: A Reminiscence Room

We have created a number of 'reminiscence rooms' within Jewish Care. These rooms – which are unique to our project, but which could be created by anyone in any space or corner – were decorated and furnished as rooms in the 1930s might have been. For example, one of the rooms has a scullery. It includes an old butler's sink, a wooden draining board, a 'meat safe,' and a dresser on which assorted china is displayed. A mangle stands in a corner of the scullery and a scrubbing board, tongs and zinc tub – once used to boil the washing – are also there. In the sitting room area are flying ducks, a 'Peach Mirror,' a Bakelite telephone, an old radio, and a television set.

49. A Reminiscence Room can contain a wide range of familiar items, including wedding dresses, menorahs, and a *genzunder*. Michael Sobell Community Centre.

Another reminiscence room furnished as a fine sitting room includes a fire screen, large wardrobe, red velvet curtains, and articles of clothing such as floral pinnies, *gutkas*, corsets, and a variety of hats and handbags. Most of the exhibits and decorations are original and the shelves are lined with artefacts from a past era such as perfume bottles, cameras, chocolate wrappers, household items, tickets and newspapers.

These rooms are used for all kinds of discussion and members love the aura of the past that has been revived in our rooms. The walls are decorated with old paintings, marriage certificates, and photographs of family gatherings, classroom scenes, seaside outings, and so on. Some of the photographs are originals and some are copies.

Because these rooms are examples of styles gone by, their use is not restricted to older people. We encourage children to come and see our exhibits and hear first-hand accounts of life in former times. Groups of carers from abroad have visited our reminiscence rooms. Recently, Prince Charles spent 15 minutes with us closely examining artefacts, photographs and mementoes relating to his own family.

50. Prince Charles visiting Jeanie Rosefield's Reminiscence Class at the Michael Sobell Community Centre.

Appendix B
Topic Boxes

Jeanie Rosefield conceived the idea of topic boxes. Pat Stanton and Anne Futter produced them.

Why do Topic Boxes help?
It is not easy for a group leader to stimulate conversation in a situation where she/he knows little or nothing about the topic concerned. A topic box gives even the most inexperienced facilitator a lead into a discussion.

How do you make a Topic Box?

1 Choose any Topic, for example, 'wintertime'. Write a list of questions relating to the topic and try them out on a group. It does not matter if the answers to questions are not 100 per cent correct; this, in itself, promotes discussion.

2 Collect artefacts relevant to the topic: long johns or Wintergreen Rub – used to cure rheumatism – might be relevant here. Second-hand shops, specialist shops and junk shops are all valuable sources of material.

3 Collect old newspaper articles and advertisements. These can be obtained from the Newspaper Library at Colindale in North West London, or bought from specialist shops or junk shops, and are also available on the Internet. Humorous articles are particularly popular.

4 Group members themselves might be able to contribute by bringing in old letters, bills and documents – even kitchen utensils – that can go into the boxes. Old photographs, which can be copied and laminated, are wonderful triggers for discussion.

5 Make a list of the contents of the boxes and ask anyone borrowing the boxes to guard them carefully and return them intact. The material in these boxes is often unique and cannot easily be replaced.

6 It took three years to make 64 topic boxes. Finding original material takes time and effort.

Appendix C
Reminiscence Action Plan

New Clothes

INTRODUCTION

'My husband hired a morning suit to go to a wedding, and my father told him that he had his morning suit made in Saville Row for his wedding in 1933 for 15 guineas! Do you remember the cost of a suit in that period?'

1 'Did people you know mainly hire clothes for special occasions, or did they make them, buy them or have them made?'

2 'Did you usually get your new clothes when you were children at the time of Jewish festivals?'

3 'Were there special fashions for teenagers, or did they wear the same as adults?'

4 'Do you remember these relics from the past – what were they? Liberty bodices, spats, galoshes, crombies, seamed stockings? Tell us about them.'

5 'I'd love to know what people wore in the 1920s and 1930s. Can you describe the fashions? What was your favourite outfit?'

CONCLUSION

'Probably we'll all be wearing disposable paper clothes in a few years!'

123

Make Up
INTRODUCTION

'I've just read in the *Sunday Times* that Nigella Lawson has discovered that she likes loose powder – it just shows how fashions in make-up come and go. What sort of make-up – if any – did you use in your young days?'

1 'Do you remember the beautiful powder boxes designed by Strattons?'

2 'What was the most popular perfume – and was it your favourite?' (For example, *Soie de Paris*).

3 'How old were you when your parents allowed you to wear make-up?'

4 'Were you considered "cheap" if you wore a lot of make-up?'

5 'What about ear-piercing, nose-piercing, painted toenails and glittery designs on finger nails – how would that have gone down?'

6 'Was there a shortage of make-up in the War? How did you get round this – did you improvise with other materials and dyes?'

7 'Did the men use toiletries, for example, after-shave, deodorants, hair gel, as they do now?' (For example, Brylcreem).

CONCLUSION

'I wonder what future generations will dream up?'

Crime

INTRODUCTION

'Everyone says it's not wise to walk about alone in the dark. Was it like that when you were young?'

1 'If it was safer to walk around alone at night, why do you think that was?' (For example, more pedestrians because fewer people had cars; very few possessions, therefore less robbery; close knit communities.)

2 'Were there more policemen on the beat?'

3 'Were you aware of the gangster underworld? Did you or your family know (or know of) any gangsters?'

4 'Were any of you a victim of muggings?'

5 'Do you think that crime was as bad but the media didn't publicise it in the same way?'

6 'How did your parents feel about your staying out after dark?'

7 'Do you think the government of today is dealing with crime in the right way?'

CONCLUSION
'Perhaps things go in cycles. Let's hope our great-grandchildren will be able to walk about safely in the streets of London.'

Lights and Lighting
INTRODUCTION
'We've just modernised our kitchen and were told the latest "must have" is spotlights. What was the fashion in lighting when you were young?'

1 'When you were children were your homes lit by electricity, gas or paraffin lamps?'

2 'Do you remember the gas streetlights – did the lamplighters come to your street?'

3 'Where did you go to buy lamps and light fittings?'

4 'Did you light *Shabbat* candles in your family?'

5 'How did you manage in the blackout during the War?' (When were torches introduced? Nightlights? Sing the song 'I'm going to get lit up when the lights go on in London.')

6 'Do you remember the "peasouper" fogs? What did they use to light up the police who were directing traffic in these fogs?' (For example, flares).

CONCLUSION
'It's amazing to read in the papers that with all our modern technology there have been several total blackouts recently in Los Angeles and Delhi.'

Potatoes

INTRODUCTION
'I've just been to the supermarket to buy potatoes and I'm confused by all the choices. Was it always like that or was it just 'a pound of potatoes please' at the corner shop, and you got what they gave you?'

1 'Were potatoes a major part of your diet when you were children or did you have a balanced diet of meat and two vegetables?'

2 'Did you associate special ways of cooking potatoes on *Shabbat* or Jewish festivals?' (For example, potato strudel, *latkes*; introduce discussion about recipes.)

3 'Did you have powdered potato during the War or could you get the real thing?'

4 'Did you go to the fish and chip shop often, or was it a special treat?'

5 'What about potato crisps – when were they introduced? Do you remember the little blue salt bag?'

6 'Did you have an allotment where you grew your own potatoes?'

CONCLUSION
'Perhaps for the next generation it will all be genetically modified potatoes – let's hope that they are not a health hazard.'

Appendix D
Some Topics for Reminiscence

51. Sharing a story with the reminiscence group at the Michael Sobell Community Centre.

1 Potatoes and what you did with them.

2 New clothes: when did you buy them?

3 Why you are glad you are not young any more.

4 Fashions that have shocked and enraged.

5 Snacks and eating in the street.

6 Vice is the spice of life: boxing, betting and gambling.

7 Wearing make-up: when was it allowed?

8 Manners and the changing ideas about good manners.

9 Favourite funny stories.

10 Big bands.

11 The first time you saw the sea.

12 Dressing to kill.

13 Much loved music.

14 What part did religion play in your lives?

15 Housing and homes.
16 New clothes.
17 Your first date.
18 Your first day at school.
19 Your last day at school.
20 Finding a job.
21 Who went on strike?
22 Cinema and entertainment.
23 Cleaning the house.
24 Jewellery and the jewellery shops.
25 When was your 'golden era'?
26 Holidays with or without pay.
27 The gramophone and the part it played in life before the television.
28 Having a baby.
29 Royalty today and yesterday.
30 Fashion when you were young.
31 War and evacuation.
32 Entertainment during the War.
33 Weddings.
34 Wintertime.
35 Personal hygiene.
36 Furniture and furnishing the home.
37 The games you played.
38 Life without a telephone.
39 Life before the television.
40 Keeping cool and smelling sweet.
41 The world of work
42 Communication: how you used to keep in touch.
43 Youth clubs.
44 Food and eating habits.
45 Street smells.
46 Street sounds.
47 Jobs that no longer exist.
48 Rationing.
49 Cleaning the house.
50 Gender issues: the difference between attitudes toward girls and boys.
51 Life's regrets.
52 Something you were proud of doing.

52. Everyday objects can trigger memories at the Michael Sobell Community Centre.

53 Travelling abroad.

54 School days.

55 Immigration.

56 Stars of stage and screen.

57 Home remedies: did they work?

58 Teatime.

59 Eating out, and Lyons Corner Houses.

Glossary of Useful Yiddish and Hebrew Words

Bar mitzvah	Religious coming of age; rite of passage into manhood
Bagel	Bread roll with a hole in the middle – boiled and then baked
Boobeles	Pancakes for Passover
Borscht	Beetroot soup
Broigus	To be angry; a quarrel
Bubbeleh	Term of affection for people of all ages: literally, 'little grandmother'
Bunkus	Small glass bulbs
Chanukah	Festival of Lights: commemorating the rededication of the Temple during the Maccabean period
Chanukiah	Candelabra; specifically used for Chanukah
Chazan	Cantor
Cheder (pl. chedorim)	Hebrew school
Chemslers	Pancakes for Passover
Cholent	Meat, bean and potato stew prepared before *Shabbat*
Chometz	Leavened bread
Chrayne	Horseradish
Chupah	Wedding canopy
Chuts	Dutch Jews

Davern	To pray in a Jewish manner, rocking to and fro
Die gute stube	The front room ('the good room')
Flak	Tart
Frummer	A religious or observant Jew
Ganef	Cheater, thief
Gatkes	Underwear (for men); Long Johns
Gelt	Money
Gezunder	Chamber pot
Glarneys	Marbles
Goy	A person who is not Jewish
Grieven	Hard pieces of rendered chicken fat
Gutkas	Boys' underwear ('combinations')
Hackmesser	Hammer, a meat chopper
Hamantashen	Triangular pastry filled with poppy seed, raisins and honey, made on the festival of Purim
Hand zu fuss	Hand to foot (a type of sleeping arrangement)
Heim	Home, homeland
Heimish	To have a Jewish flavour; to be homely
'Kann er macht ein leben?'	'Can he make a living?'
Kappel	Skull cap
Kirchel	A plain biscuit
Kishkes	Intestines
Kopf zu fuss	Head to foot (a type of sleeping arrangement)
Kosher	In accordance with Jewish dietary laws
Knippel	Money that has been saved and hidden away
Kurve	Loose woman
Latkes	Potato pancakes
Litvaks	Lithuanian Jews
Lobus	Bad boy
Lockshen	Noodles
Lum dust	Granulated sugar
Mandelach	Almond biscuits

Mezzuzah	A religious symbol containing a hand-written scroll which is affixed to the door post
Matzo	Unleavened bread
Melamed	Man of learning
Mazeltov	Good luck
Menorah	A seven-armed candelabra
Metze-er	A bargain
Moishe	The name traditionally given to traders (the Yiddish version of Moses)
Nudden	Dowry
'Nisht in front of die kinder'	'Not in front of the children'
Nosh	Snack
Parana	Feather-filled cover resembling a duvet
Pesach	Passover; commemorating the Exodus from Egypt
Pflaumen	Prunes
Platzel	Hard-baked bread roll
Polacks	Polish Jews
Pooch	Poultry feathers used for bedding or cushions
Purim	Festival of Lots; commemorating the triumph of the Jews of Persia over Haman
'Redden nicht Yiddish mit mir'	'Don't speak Yiddish with me'
Reebazen	Grater
Rosh Hashanah	Jewish New Year
Rozinkes und mandelen	Almonds and raisins
Schlufbank	Pull-out bed
Schlepper	Somebody who dragged people into a shop or up to a stall, encouraging them to buy
Schmaltz	Grease; fat
Seder	Passover meal
Serrata	Oil cloth used to cover kitchen tables

133

Shvitz bad	Steam bath
Schwitz	Sweat
Shabbat	Sabbath
Shadchan	Matchmaker
Shavuot	Festival of Weeks; anniversary of the giving of the Torah
Sheitel	Wig (worn by Orthodox women after marriage)
Shidduch	Marital match
Schmutter	Rag; anything worthless
Succot	Festival to commemorate the wanderings of the Jewish people in the wilderness after the Exodus from Egypt
Talmud Torah	Hebrew school; study of the Torah
Tanzen mit Vanzen	Dancing with bedbugs
Tchoochele	Darling
Torah	Jewish Bible; the Pentateuch
Uberdeck	Feather-filled cover resembling a duvet
Vanna	Zinc bath
Vanzen	Bedbugs
'Weibe, weibe, die beste is here'	'Women, women, we've got the best'
Wurst	Kosher sausage
Yiddish	Jewish
Yom Kippur	Day of Atonement

Note on old currency

Before British currency became decimalised, the pound was made up of 20 shillings (20s), and each shilling consisted of twelve pennies (written as 1d, 2d, etc.). Pennies were also further broken down into half pennies (ha'pennies) and farthings (worth a quarter of a penny). A guinea was 21s.

There are a couple of slang terms in the text: a bob was the nickname for a shilling; a threepenny bit was a coin worth 3d; tupenny and tuppence means 2d; penn'orth means a penny's worth.